In Shetland

In Shetland

Tales from The Last Bookshop

Tom Morton

A Looderhorn Book

First published in 2017
Looderhorn Books
A division of Tom Morton Publishing
The Last Bookshop
Northmavine Manse
Hillswick
Shetland ZE2 9RW

IN SHETLAND

A catalogue record for this book is available from the National
Library of Scotland, Edinburgh

ISBN 978-0-9563085-4-2

Versions of some pieces in this book were previously published in
*60 North Magazine, Shetland Life, The Shetland Times,
shetland.org, Living Orkney, Scottish Memories, The Scots
Magazine, The Scotsman, The Scottish Review, Caught by the
River, Whisky Magazine* and *iScot.*

Book formatted by www.bookformatting.co.uk.

Contents

Tom Morton was born in Carlisle, England, to Scottish parents making a desperate and ultimately unsuccessful run north for the border before his birth. He was educated in Troon and Glasgow, and has worked in newspapers, broadcasting, magazines, fundamentalist evangelism, knitwear, rock'n'roll, tourism, PR and the whisky industry. He is married and lives in the Shetland village of Quidawick, proud capital of Ramnavine, where he runs The Last Bookshop in The World. He has five children, five grandchildren, five bicycles, two kayaks and a dog.

Last

This is the last place. There is nowhere else to go.

Once again we celebrate the
Headland's huge, carin-studded fall
into the Sea.

This is the last place. There is nowhere else to go.

For we have walked the jewelled beaches
at the feet of the final cliffs
of all Man's wanderings.

This is the last place

There is nowhere else to go.

Lew Welch: *The Song Mt. Tamalpais Sings*

Lost

I am not lost. I know where I am. I am in Shetland.

Not 'on' Shetland. This was drummed into me by Rayleen, a former editor of *The Shetland Post*. Well, bellowed into me, at that time a fumbling know-all soothmoother reporter. A lot of those passed through the paper's portals.

"You may be ON a boat," she said, very loudly, on the single, entirely memorable occasion I submitted copy stating that someone was currently *on* Shetland. Or that the situation *on* Shetland had deteriorated. Or something. "Or you may be ON holiday. Or for all I know and care ON DRUGS. But as far as I can tell you are neither vacationing nor floating. Nor are you in some kind of pharmacological fugue. But you are currently *IN* SHETLAND, and don't you forget it."

And I never have forgotten. Tonight I am in the part of the Shetland Mainland called Ramnavine. In Quidawick, to be precise.

In Shetland. Need I mention that it is never 'The Shetlands'? This is a singular place.

The walk, this November night, is from sea to sea, Aest Ayre to West, beach to beach, North Sea to Atlantic. The storm is gathering its forces in the sky, which is moon-blue behind heaving, shifting cloud. The wind is moving round from north-west to south-east, leaving the big, Atlantic waves crashing onto the West Ayre, over the stile and across 200 metres of field. I am not going there, not after dark. Rocks come hurtling through the shifting air on a night like this. It's dangerous.

And this is nothing. Mild, compared to the hurricane that deposited a boulder on the roof of the Karaness lightkeeper's house, on a clifftop 200 feet above the sea. A stone so big it took three men to move it. And that is a mere piece of nature's tricksy bluster, compared to the tsunami, the '200-year-wave' they say explains the line of sofa-sized rocks in a ragged line along those same cliffs.

Or it could be a 100-year-wave. In which case it's overdue and might arrive tonight. Oh well.

Nothing, a mere breeze. Nevertheless I am wrapped up, be-hatted, Goretex-clad and engloved. For this little wander. You can't be too careful. It's cold, the wind reinforcing the chill, but not like the killing temperatures of January. I think of those who have died, overheated from a hall dance, walking in shirtsleeves, feeling the blessed relief, the drying sweat. Wandering too far, stumbling onto the weathered hill, taking a short cut home, or just wandering, waiting for the drink to wear off. Cooling, cooling until they go too far to ever come back, and the cold takes them. Lost.

I walk this route every night, hauled by one small, enthusiastic dog, pulling an old, large dying one. I am not lost. I am in the village which is my home. I know every inch of the track, the road, the path behind one beach, the Aest Ayre, where the waves are simply restless, waiting for the new direction of wind to pile them up in St Olaf's Bay, into Quida Wick, Quida Bay, and then send great welts of water piling into the semi-circle of houses which includes our own.

I pass the cemetery, built in an exact circle on a promontory of dry land within a tidal marsh. Birds, waders, love this place in autumn and spring. Redshanks, lapwings, sandpipers. Tonight, faintly in the sound of wind and wave, I can hear a lone redwing, one of thousands migrating south at this time of year. They travel by night, seeking companionship in that sad, mournful keening. It's one of the loneliest sounds in the world.

This is a very old graveyard, no longer used, but maintained carefully, like all Shetland cemeteries, because of its Pictish stones and Commonwealth war graves. Almost all Shetland cemeteries have war graves. The lost-at-sea, found on an island shore. Once, many years, ago, when we first came to Quidawick, I felt nervous walking past the long, close-cropped grass pathway. Now, even the unearthly glint of two eyes, belonging to a cat sitting on one of the gateposts, cannot frighten me. I know the cat. Raymond the fat tortoiseshell, scourge of curlews and the rarer whimbrels. A nasty piece of work. I know these graves. There are no ghosts here.

But there are stories. And one it's difficult, this blustery night, not to think of, as Raymond turns his brilliantly fluorescent gaze on us, and Dexter the Staffordshire-sheepdog strains, silently, to get at him. Raymond and Dexter are not friends.

Her name was Katherine Jonesdochter (note the Icelandic, female-succession name) who was strangled, and then burned in a vat of pitch, the last woman accused of witchcraft to suffer this horrific fate in Scotland. The sentence was carried out on the hill above Scalloway, Shetland's old capital and now second to Lerwick in status and size. But Katherine was a Ramnavine woman, a poor soul who stood accused of 'conversing, keeping company and lying with the deil' over 40 years, regularly, especially 'at Halloween and Holy Cross Day', and seeing trowies, the strange, troll-like fairies of the north, dancing in the very kirkyard I walk past each night, and several times a day.

She was executed on 2 October 1616. On the 400th anniversary of her death, just a few weeks ago, I walked past the Quidawick graveyard as usual. On that occasion there wasn't even a cat's eyes to check my stride. Raymond had business elsewhere, doubtless exterminating rare wildlife.

Tonight I pass Da Noost, the ancient Hanseatic trading post and former pub that is now a wildlife sanctuary, home to abandoned seals and otters. The great wooden pile of the St Rognvald Hotel, its windows pulsating with light and sound from the disco within, Steve Earle, Lynryd Skynyrd, Status Quo. There's shouting and I can smell the fag-reek from unsteady bodies outside, the eternally exiled smokers. What would poor old Katherine Jonesdochter make of it all, I wonder, the clumsy shoogling of bodies, the clinches and stumbles, the shouts and flirting, the blunt groping?

Down past the Tarry Shed, now restored by Patrick, manager to rock and roll royalty, as an art gallery and apartment for his part-time residence here. He has found himself in Shetland too, but he was never lost in this place. It was always a destination, a certainty. For all the 60s' tales of lost festivals, gigs, bands and indeed years, of ornate religion, of long journeys through India, of drugs and money and all the vintage wildness of major league rock'n'roll, Patrick is one of the least lost people I have ever met.

The shop is opposite, closed of course. The Quidawick Stores. I am in there every day, or nearly. Bread, milk, wellington boots, buckets, salt fish, reestit mutton, browning fruit, soft vegetables. We are very far away here. I remember one friend, bought up on the northernmost island of Shetland, Unst, telling me how, until he was 14, he thought bananas were black. Another acquaintance reminiscing about how she could only get olive oil on prescription from the chemist in Lerwick. Now our shop has sun-dried tomatoes, and terrible 'Lifestyle' brand cash-and-carry hummus. Though you can buy chickpeas, some extra virgin oil, tahini, lemon and garlic and make your own.

The beach is rattling and whispering, its small stones allegedly dumped here back in the 19th century to provide a suitable place for the drying of herring. We stick to the grass behind the rock armouring, the coastal protection put in place in the 1970s after a major flood which saw seawater in our house up to the top of the kitchen Rayburn; we pass a giant iron anchor, more than eight feet tall and five wide, salvaged by Ernest the Engineer from a sunken cruiser out in the bay. He is a man of awesome skills, Ernest, who has built boats, traction engines and whose specialised forged tools are exported all over the world. Nowadays, for fun, he makes all his own clothes and shoes, and dresses like an extremely well-turned-out gamekeeper. He used to be a gun dealer and sometimes you'll hear enormous bangs from Quidawick Ness, where he is out with his old muzzle-loader, eradicating the rabbit population.

Ernest and a team of blacksmiths imported specially from Yorkshire once hand-forged an anchor as big as this enormous First World War one, when they were all old enough to know better. It was the last anchor to be hand-forged in Britain in the 20th century. I pass an iron sculpture of flowers, strange and beautiful, made by Ernest's daughter Philomena. I know it is there, but I cannot see it.

It is lost in the shadows.

Our house is almost in the sea, a mere one metre above high tide mark and perhaps five from where the sea peaks. On the beach, really. With the right combination of tide and wind the waves will slop over the armouring and cover the cars, sometimes foaming right up to the front door.

You should never buy a second-hand car from Shetland, not if you care about rust. And we all care about it, we should care. Rust never sleeps, as the great Neil says. Shetland is where rust never even takes the shortest of naps. This is where salt-accelerated corrosion can savage a Toyota Hi-Lux to death in a few short years. I remember selling a boat to a fellow who reversed his two-year-old pickup down a slipway to haul the old Shetland Model onto its trailer. Deeper and deeper he went, until the water was lapping at the truck's windows.

Wasn't he worried about the salt water's effect on his vehicle?

"Nah, nah boy," he replied. "It's leased and it's going back next week."

And that time, not long after arriving, when I bought a Fiat Panda 4X4 from a ruthlessly exploitative local dealer. It never worked properly, failing to start on demand, cutting out for no apparent reason, smelling peculiar and rusting at a ferocious rate, even for a Fiat. Though its aroma wasn't as spectacularly awful as the decrepit Mitsubishi Colt bought from a fisherman, held together with bungee cords and, after a desperate inspection, hiding three mummified mackerel underneath the back seat.

I stuttered into the Hogganfield filling station in Lerwick with the Panda for petrol one day, and was paying when the cashier shook her head and said: "I never thought I'd see that car again." There was a long pause. "Not after they pulled it out of the harbour." I made the garage I'd bought it from take the horrible thing back and refund all our cash.

Now I carefully cross the cattle grid, Dexter pulling as usual and old Rug, the nearly-dead St Bernard, tottering, if a St Bernard can totter, across the planks laid just for her ageing feet to find. The lights of the house are yellow, welcoming. Inside, I know there is good whisky and I can smell the acrid fumes of peat burning in the downstairs stove. The smell of smouldering turf is a potent madeleine of memory, loaded with images of my years in Shetland. The peat-ash, cabbage and stewed tea aroma of a Hjalda Voe cottage. The mid-winter bubbling of water in a back boiler. The staggering around Quidawick, many years ago, before I ever thought of living here, a bottle of Bushmills in hand as the Northern Lights, Da Mirrie Dancers, shimmered and rippled across the winter sky above, the pungency of peatsmoke marking the memory forever.

This place. This place I've found. I'm heart-lost in love for it. I hear the sign creaking, whining as it oscillates on its hinges. It catches the ochre illumination from the kitchen window as it swings, but it's hard to read. I know what it says, anyway. I painted it myself. Last Books. Furthest north, lurking to catch the bibliophile unawares, here at the Edge of The World: *Ultima Thule*.

And I open the door to my house, my business, my way of life, my being. I go inside, shutting the storm out, unleashing the dogs, shrugging off my coat.

It's time to begin. It's time to sit down, next to the Rayburn, among my books – although they could be your books too; all you have to do is buy them. Everything's for sale. Or nearly everything – and tell my stories. You don't have to listen.

But seeing as you're here…

Books

That's what the notice says. Last Books.

Books, even in this digitised era of pixelated 'web content', have lasted, will last. Libraries, collections, bookshops: they're the difference between human beings and beats. To some – the hurried, the hipsters, the glossy thumb-twitchers of tablet and smartphone – there may be a desperation, a sadness in hoarding, owning, selling lumps of paper and cardboard, but it's not just about data, information. It's about wisdom, art, knowledge. Books are nurtured, caressed, underlined, commented on, abused. Sometimes I think they're as close to living things as makes no difference. Or at least, the recently dead. Last wills, testaments. At any rate, this is one of the last places you'll find a sad old man willing to exchange real, printed books for cash. No cards, no cheques, no Bitcoins. Money.

The sign doesn't say 'Bookshop'. That would contravene planning law, as The Bookshop at The Edge of The World is actually an old, rambling house called Da Kirk o' da Shun, full of forehead-crunching doors, unexpected steps and rickety shelves that sway in the wind. Well, it's the wooden panelling on the walls that occasionally flutters in a big gust, sending the shelves into a mild rocking motion which can make you think you're at sea.

And in sense, you are. This is the remote north of Shetland's biggest island, which is called Mainland, because it's the main bit of land. As opposed to 'the mainland', which is Scotland, some 200 miles south. Locally referred to as 'sooth'. The winds – big, frequently hurricane force – come howling in from the Atlantic or the North Sea; Shetland is the crossroads, the receptacle for all sorts of driftwood, detritus, flotsam and jetsam. Things get washed up here. All sorts of things.

Me, for instance.

I escaped, first of all, from my mother's womb, only to find I was in the wrong place.

"What, in the name of William Wallace (as played, dripping with woad, by Mel Gibson)," I said – there are multiple witnesses – "am I doing in Carlisle?"

Carlisle Maternity Hospital, to be precise, which was, and I assume still is, a fine place. I have never seen it as an adult. I have been to, and through Carlisle itself many times, and never without feeling a deep swell of anger. Why, I demand of myself, of my late mother, and (rarely) of my father, who is in his 80s and even more irritable than in his always-easily-annoyed prime: WHY DIDN'T YOU CROSS THE BORDER AND HAVE ME IN SCOTLAND?

Nine miles. Nine miles, after all, is all that separated me from the sound of bagpipes and a restorative suckling of haggis juice welcoming me as a True Caledonian. Nine miles further north and years of vilification from schoolmates, a misguided attempt to support the English football team, and a deep physical aversion to kilts might have been avoided.

I know now that I am not alone. Carlisle Maternity is the birthplace of thousands, tens of thousands of would-have-been Scots from Wigtownshire, Dumfriesshire and other southern outposts of Tartanland. Nationality comes second to health and safety, pride to proper anaesthetics and midwifery, even if there has to be a Cumbrian accent involved. But while others have settled into their hybrid lives, their birth certificates denying their love for Alex Salmond, their willingness to overlook Nicola Sturgeon's haircut, their genetic attraction towards deep fried Mars Bars – I have not. For me there has always been a desire to go north, to go further north, as far as it is possible to get, even to the very edges of Scotland, which is, after all, my world.

And here I am. The Last Bookseller in The Last Bookshop in the Last Place before Scotland slips into the sea and Arctic climes beckon. Well, the Faroe Islands, where they eat puffins and slaughter whales. And then eat them.

At least it's not Carlisle.

*** *** ***

That sign: Books. Or, I suppose, 'Books.' Note the capital 'B'. It could mean a number of things. It could be a simple proclamation that books exist. A gentle reminder to the passing motorist, cyclist, pedestrian or low-flying helicopter pilot of a form of communication which involves paper, text, and card. Not some flourish of pixels on a screen. Objects, tactile and physical, organic, soft, prone to damage and rot. Cheap or ferociously expensive. but never worthless. Human outpourings of anguish and joy, learned irrelevance and breathtaking genius. What people leave behind. Pieces of humanity.

And items of trade. Books to buy, books to sell, books to trade. Volumes. Volumes of volumes.

The truth is, the sign means simply that there are books lurking in the big old house, that somebody (me) is likely to be found and is willing to receive visitors, potential customers, and exchange some of those books for money. Apart from that, I don't really advertise, and few people actually respond to it. Apart from one or two friends and neighbours who take it as an indication that I'm in and willing to provide coffee, tea and the plain chocolate digestive biscuits I like. Or possibly a dram.

Some of my local acquaintances will browse the shelves, occasionally borrowing a book that's taken their fancy, or asking if they can listen to one of the several hundred vinyl LPs and singles that I also… own. 'Stock' seems the wrong word. There are guitars, too, old guitars for strumming, twanging and occasionally seducing, at a price, someone who didn't know he or she just had to own a 1960 Harmony Sovereign or a 1972 Fylde Orsino. I mean, almost everything here in The Last Bookshop is for sale, at a price. Even I'm for sale, sort of. Abashed, I will admit that those paintings, the little sculptures, the collages featuring old Ordnance Survey maps, yes, they're all mine. I made them. I will sell you one, if you like. Or a book, a guitar, a record, a record player. Something from the museum of Lost Audio.

Then I can buy other things.

Because selling books and records isn't really the point. Money is necessary, but it's not the end, the be all and end all. Being here is the point. First and foremost, to be among books. The smell of books. And peat smoke, from the cast iron stove, which of course doesn't really provide the kind of humidity-controlled environment in which – some rather valuable – volumes should be kept. But then, as I said, this is a sort-of-bookshop designed, first and foremost, for my comfort and pleasure.

The coffee... I offer free coffee to everyone who comes in, all my, well, customers. Or potential customers. Sometimes you have to take the long view, cultivating someone for weeks or even months before they decide to buy that vintage copy of *Biggles Goes West* for, oh, 50 pence. The coffee is not to everyone's taste. Some people prefer instant, any form of instant, to my Beanshop-of-Perth Blend 67, V60 filtered, super strong delight. I can and will do an Aeropress, if I really like you, but don't ask for a cappuccino. I only release my inner Barista on the second-hand Rancilio Silvia machine to appease my own frothy desires.

And there's music, of course. I mustn't forget The Museum of Lost Audio. The giant, 1960s KEF loudspeakers, the ancient Quad valve amplifier, painted eggshell hospital blue, which glows orange and smells of burning pylons. The manual Linn Sondek record deck, made in Glasgow 30 years ago by redundant shipyard workers. I also have a selection of other vintage sound equipment (cassette recorders, radios, reel-to-reel tape machines, even the occasional Minidisc or 8-Track) most of it for sale. Probably. At the right price. To people who seem deserving of ownership. I mean, you have to be discriminating in this business. Did I say 'business?' My wife, Susan, says it's a shed.

"It's the ultimate shed, Tom," she announced during her first formal visit. She had been before, obviously, as it's her house too, but I didn't actually formalise the retail nature, so to speak, of the room (formerly the minister's study) until about a year ago. "It's a male thing. You've got your books, your records, your guitars, your horrible pieces of smelly hot audio stuff. You're happy as a pig in shit."

"Why do women not have sheds?" I wasn't issuing any denials. She was right. This is a kind of shed, only with a public aspect. And I can claim the electricity against tax. Or some of it.

"Women don't have sheds because they have houses," replied Susan, crisply. "Homes. There's no need to escape to secret little worlds where they can..tinker. Play games. Actually," – and she glanced around, at the comfortable old couch, the ample floorspace – "I'm surprised you don't have a train set in here. Or a Scalextric. There's room."

I folded my arms and thought for a minute. Scalextric. The very word ignited a hitherto ignored flame in my multi-fuel heart. Model racing cars. A childhood spent bemoaning the pathetic oval which was all I ever owned, longing for a figure of eight, a lap counter, that thing that made racing car engine noises. I'd already been thinking about model railways. Hornby Dublo. I mean, I have grandchildren, who admittedly don't live in Shetland, but still. In truth, my ambitions extend to something more extreme.

"You're quite right," I said. "But what I really fancy is an O-gauge system for the garden, you know, like Neil Young has. Neil Young the Canadian singer songwriter, not Neil o'da Flitterwicks." (Neil o'da (of the) Flitterwicks (his house), also surnamed Young, is a well-known local crofter and mild-mannered ex-hippy with a tendency to wax garrulous on the subject of the Beeching Cuts and the importance of steam in British culture.)

The truth is, I do make a few small compromises, some gestures towards appeasing the little gods of retail. Tourists do come, a few of them, a select few, people for whom holidays mean, at least partially, shopping. Who seek a native environment, an exchange with the locals, that they can take away as a memory of 'the real Shetland.' So I have things I can give them in exchange for money. Souvenirs. A few paintings, photographs, not to mention bits of local knitwear. Marjolein Bennersdottir's socks, for example, hand-knitted with love and a passion for a tradition handed down from her grandfather. Yes, grandfather. Because here at The Edge of The

World, knitting is and always has been an activity unrestricted by gender expectations.

Lara Stenderson's stunning lace-knit shawls, soft and fragrant with natural lanolin, undyed, priceless and yes, pricey. Each one takes her weeks, sometimes months of work. Will anybody buy one? Does it matter?

Not really. They exist. Young men and women in Shetland are learning how to make them, so they always, I hope, will exist. Just as long as I can continue to walk or cycle along the seashore road from Quidawick to Gurnafirth, past otters and sheep, seals and skuas, crafters and grafters, and immigrant capitalist running dogs; not to mention native running sheepdogs that'll nip at your ankles in an enthusiastic and blood-extracting manner.

As long as I can, in a purely self-indulgent manner, fire up the coffee machine, settle down into the worn leather of my salvaged-from-a-skip armchair having let the Linn's Ittok arm settle its stylus with a soft, comfortable 'thunk!' onto a mint example of Charlie Parker: *The Savoy Years*, and luxuriate in that warm, wondering, wandering sound, all wrapped up in the aromas of ageing books, brewing java, hot valve amplifier, the sweet tang of wool, and, if I can be bothered lighting the stove, the pungency of burning peat.

On my first day of official shopkeeping, with the Last Books sign newly painted and creaking, Admiral-Benbow-style in the fairly mild breeze, I did exactly that (only with Miles's *Kind of Blue* providing a meditative dose of cool), sipped a cup of Blend 67 and pondered the future: it would be nice if a few customers of the right type (clean, well-educated, travellers from far distant lands with great stories to tell, laden with cash, their feet carefully wiped on the mat) did pop in and buy, say, the £50 signed George Mackay Brown first edition, my specially and expensively copied Blau reproduction 17th century maps at £20, or the cushioned leather *Complete Works of Longfellow* (£40). That would be a nice way to start. A bit of a return on my various investments. In books I'd read, caressed and inhaled, or maps I'd had (very expensively) copied onto hand-made paper, probably not very wisely.

On the other hand, George Mackay Brown, just a few weeks

13

before his death, had signed a copy of *Beside The Ocean of Time*, his last book, for me in his Stromness living room. A room in which he had served me an enormous Old Orkney whisky. Could I really sell something so personal, so precious with memory? I sat for a few more minutes, had another sip of blacker-than-black coffee, then grabbed a pencil and rubber and went over to the glass cabinet containing 'Rare and First Editions – Fondling on Request'. A few seconds later, the final book by God's favourite Orcadian was £100.

No sane person would buy it at that price. But then I remembered that second-hand bookshops were magnets for the insane and the obsessed. I rubbed out £100 and gently wrote in £200. Some memories are priceless. And some are just prohibitively expensive.

The Bookshop at The Edge of The World, The Repository of Last Books, The Final Shelf, Tom's Last Case... you choose... is not, of course, simply a bookshop. It is a time machine, an instant Starship (but not Starbucks) Enterprise, a means of transport to the furthest outposts of the universe, or possibly the island of Unst (two islands up from me; the northernmost lump of land in this disunited Kingdom). It is a repository of knowledge, of laughter, tears and thrills. And of course there's the music (basically, the record collections of myself and my friend Francisco; I swapped him a bottle of Lebanese Chateau Musar for 250 rather damp LPs he had in his garage), plus, for pennies, a few of the thousands of promotional CDs sent to me by record companies over the years. A few of the thousands of, not crap, but to me unlistenable CDs sent by record companies. Once, I was an arbiter of taste. Until I realised my arbitration was becoming cussed and contrary, my likes and dislikes set in stone too many years ago. You like Green Day? There's a popular CD from that diminutive beat combo for 10 pence. Play it with my blessing. You will need to be blessed, for it is a demonic pile of poo, grating and nasty. But it's worth 10p, I'm sure. All right, I'll take five. Och, take it away, why don't you? Turn it into an ashtray.

As well as the books, the contents of the Museum of Lost Audio, the guitars, pictures, socks, scarves, shawls and maps... the quality stuff... I do, I confess, have a host of cheap souvenirs too, like keyrings, postcards and God help me, mousemats featuring seals, basking. And otters. Everybody loves an otter. Just don't try and cuddle one or, like Gavin Maxwell's then-youthful assistant Terry Nutkins, you could lose most of your fingers.

I do want customers, I do, as opposed to or in addition to my friends, neighbours and acquaintances. Customers will be welcomed. I may indeed offer them a coffee, if I like the cut of their jib, if they remove their wellies and their socks don't stink. But the Fawlty-esque, *Black Books*ian truth is that if I don't like the look of them, they will be invited to leave. If they pick up a book and I feel in any way uncomfortable with their touch on my possession and obsessions, I will ask them to depart. First politely, then violently. That's the kind of bookshop this is. The kind I like. I come from the Basil school, and I'm proud to have him as my alma pater: You CAN see the sea. That's it over there between the land and the sky...

So, do you want to buy a book? Sorry. That one's sold, I'm afraid. In fact go away and leave me in peace. What do you think this is? A shop?

Those hand-knits. Beautiful, aren't they? They are hugely expensive compared to the cheap imported woollies from Chinese sweatshops you get in the likes of PriMarks and Spencer, but what can I say? I love them, the way they smell so beautifully of the sea, the sky and the cleaned summer fleeces found naturally in Edge of The World sheep. I have been a hopeless habitué of knitwear shops since I came to this place, drunk on the aromas, inhaling deeply from innocent jumpers, eyed suspiciously by shopkeepers who possibly see me as some kind of pervert. But it's an aesthetic thing. A Shetland thing. Wool. Oo, as it's known.

Now, when I say 'Edge of The World', I have history on my side. I have, in point of fact, a nameless Roman Centurion on my side. A Centurion of Marines, or whatever the Roman equivalent was. He it was, doubtless weary and very seasick, who apparently reached Orkney, or Orcadia, and scrawled in his notebook (or had a slave scrawl down on some papyrus) the words "Also seen was

Thule". Also seen was The Edge of The World. By which he is thought to have meant The Shetland Isles. By which I think he meant, That's it, boys of the Cohort! No further, I don't care if there's a shadow on the horizon, we're heading back to Kirkwall for some cormorant pizza. Or something like that. Perhaps a shag (a near relative of the cormorant, eaten during World War Two in London's top restaurants as, ahem, Highland Goose).

Shetland. Britain's last outpost. Formerly known as Zetland, a name which some locals, obsessed with their Norse heritage, object to, with its buzzy overtones of Dutchness. I rather like it, actually. It carries a sense of extreme foreignness, strangeness, that 'Z'. Until the 1950s, the postal address was 'Zetland, North Britain'. Forget Scotland. And in truth, until the advent of a Scottish Parliament in Edinburgh, many Shetlanders, or Zetlanders, or Hjaltlanders if you want to go the whole Norse hog, did forget Scotland, or would rather have forgotten it. Shetland was more like some North Sea colony. A Falklands of the north. Three hundred miles from Edinburgh, 600 from London. The nearest railway station isn't actually in Bergen, Norway, as some folk like to say (that's in Thurso, Caithness). But it might as well be.

And even today, the postcodes hark back to the Zetland of yore: ZE, they all begin. ZE. The end, the final letter, the last of the UK. I like it that way. This is, after all, where I ended up. And where I found something approximating the meaning of life.

It will not have escaped your notice that The Bookshop at The Edge of The World is not just a bookshop. The souvenir-and-socks aspect reflects a desire to stock work by my neighbours, which is both a pleasure and a duty. This is a community, after all, and that brings responsibilities. Of friendship, of support, of care and concern. And of feuding, fighting and backbiting. But more of that later.

Some Shetlanders – mostly townies from Lerwick, which is more like Thurso, Wick or any other small Scottish northern town than anything else – trumpet the idea of some kind of single, proud Shetland identity, but Shetland is really a collection of communities. There are 15 or so inhabited islands, and maybe 120 (including small lumps of grass, sheep and rock) without current human habitation. This little outpost, which I shall call Ramnavine, because that is its name, is a community of communities – Quidawick, Karaness, Dollum, Viggabury, Redskerry – but most importantly, Ramnavine is almost an island in its own right, joined to the rest of the biggest Shetland island, Mainland, by the isthmus of Elsi Grind – across which the Vikings allegedly dragged their longships from the North Sea to the Atlantic and vice versa.

Ramnavine is at the very north of Mainland, beyond Brae, the sprawling feeder town for the giant Sullom Voe Oil Terminal. It possesses quite possibly – and I'm trying to be objective here – the most spectacular scenery in the whole of spectacular Shetland. The best cliffs at Karaness, the highest point (Hjalda Hill, a mass of red granite). It has volcanic outcrops, huge waterfalls, miles of deserted (and inaccessible) beaches. It has The Bookshop at The Edge of The World.

Here be Last Books.

Hangovers

Recovering from a hangover is best done in a bookshop.

I'm not talking about one of those modern hypermarkets of print, those multi-storey dispensaries of discount Pratchett and cut-price Rowling, those temples to swipe-card mammon. In fact, I hate new books. I hate their smell, the aroma of synthetic glue and chemically-treated paper. I hate what they contain, most of them, from the masturbatory driving drivel of Jeremy Clarkson to the ghost-written dribblings of Kate Moss; oh, that culture of celebrity prose! Though to dignify these clumps of processed tree with the word 'prose' is an insult to the greats, such as Sven Hassel and Shirley Conran. I'm joking of course. Conran isn't just great. She is a genius.

Nor should you be misled by the fake comfort of those city-centre Waterstones-and-their-ilk monuments to TV tie-ins and public appearances by Joan Collins, complete with botox assistant and IV drip. Those leather settees, so beloved of the homeless, and from which they are harassed by fresh-faced, polo-shirted assistants, bulging suspiciously with muscle; the aroma of ludicrously expensive coffee, the dark-stained country house fakery of the shelving, those hideously coy notes of recommendation, supposedly handwritten by those bouncy, bulky staff, the secret bookpolice.

Displaying a profoundly post-modernist command of aristocratic slang and street vernacular, Prince Charles's first foray into hard-boiled detective fiction will thrill fans of the New Royalist trend in police procedurals. Right up there

with   Zara   Phillips'   three-day-eventing   classic
Slaughterhouse Piebald...

Gwendoline, Hull branch.

All the appurtenances of high falutin', high street, high turnover bookflogging will not soothe you into a languorous state of detoxification. They are there to make you buy, both the crap and credible, but mostly the crap. That coffee is laced with secret consumerist chemicals. Those sofas contain digital relays that spout subliminal messages into your drowsy ear, insisting that you buy, immediately, Richard Hammond on Neitszche or that monobrowed fellow from Oasis on underwater archaeology. Or they whisper, authoritatively, that the new Nick Hornby is not imbecilic, word-processing-by-a-monkey-who-supports-Arsenal   rubbish,   despite what you know deep in your heart has always been true about Nick Hornby: he's a slack-nerved purveyor of complete tosh, an Anne Tyler without balls. And bald. Oh so very bald.

Old books are what you want. Used books cure hangovers. Also colds, flu, cancer loneliness, depression, male pattern hair loss, and very possibly female pattern hair loss, should such an ailment exist. Well, perhaps not entirely. But at the very least, they distract even the most old and baldy of gits from his (or her) age, alopecia and git-dom. Some books are magical, without doubt, transforming lives, causing empires to crumble. Some – most – are mindpulp, not even an opiate for the people, a cheap, short-term analgesic. Some are worse than that.

Ah, but together, in the mass, gathered, they cast a healing spell. And they smell so good. They smell like... all the wisdom in the world, all the humour, all the style, the excitement, every country, from the stinking farmyard to the seaside ozone, the city diesel to the mountaintop purity. They smell of every human emotion and condition, all the wars and celebrations, every drink and foodstuff that ever existed. Life.

The aroma of old book can range from the musky, animal odour you can find in leather bound volumes of any age, cracked open unexpectedly, leaking and leaching out cured cow from decades, sometimes hundreds of years ago. Or the slightly damp, suntan oil reek of a holiday paperback or airport special edition. John Le Carré, back from Thailand, slathered in Ambre Solaire. Then there are the multifarious skin secretions, bacteria and viruses carried by readers, and, through the years of impregnation into paper and ink, rendered not just harmless, but actually curative, in the same way diseases like smallpox can be vaccinated against through the application of a diluted variant of the disease. I admit this is a fact not entirely sustained by proven, blind-tested scientific evidence, but we all know it's true, don't we?

The first bookshop I remember was McGuigans in Troon, that slightly rundown golfing resort and commuter enclave on the Ayrshire coast. Royal Troon is the golf course used every few years for the Open championship, an opportunity for local householders to rent out their Barratt and Wimpy semi-detacheds to Pringle-sweatered American tourists for colossal sums of cash, while the householders jet off to Tenerife for the week. My first secular bookshop. Long before that, dad would take us to the Pickering and Inglis, a religious bookstore in Bothwell Street, Glasgow, to browse the uplifting missionary autobiographies or, every January, for the Bible Sale. Misprinted leather-bound lumps of India paper would be piled in cardboard cases. That was where I first saw my Uncle Victor smelling bibles, sniffing them like he was searching for some residue of cocaine, or angel dust. Not that I would have known at the time, about anything like that. Though I did like inhaling Vic decongestant, and in fact still do. What's wrong with that?

New Bibles have a glorious aroma of car seats and ink, and they even sound good – that sophisticated whistling rustle of terribly thin paper. Most of the sale Bibles had been over-inked, or printed in the wrong font, and were difficult to read as a consequence. I still have a King James version in stern all-bold print from the time, aged 11, when I was Officially Born Again, inscribed to me from my father. Earthly, not heavenly. You'd have thought a non-sale, properly printed Bible might have been appropriate for such an august occasion, but there you go. A bargain is a bargain. But now that little calfskin book smells old, slightly musty, and the India leaves are crumpled from disuse and damp, foxed and faded.

Bibles make hangovers worse, in my experience. Something to do with the bindings, and being bound by them. Best to put them aside, though they can hold great treasures, especially the burnished Sunday companions that have lived through a lifetime of someone's faith. They can be full of notes, cards, invitations, shopping lists, cries of grief and joy. You can feel guilt about trespassing on a dead man or woman's inner life. Or you can do as my long-dead grandfather, a well-known preacher in the Christian – better known as Plymouth – Brethren sect we belonged to, did: buy them and cut them up to paste requisite texts into his sermon notes, and throw the rest away. He loved The Book, but not necessarily the books. For me, it's the other way around.

Hangovers were unknown in the Brethren I grew up in, where folk simply didn't drink. The branch we belonged to was rooted in west of Scotland heavy industry and mining, and the temperance movement was always a part of that rescue-the-perishing, trophies-of-grace approach to salvation. And in places like Bellshill in Lanarkshire, among the mines and steelworks, the poverty and death – my grandfather on my dad's side was killed in an industrial mining accident when he was in his thirties, leaving his widow to bring up three children on her own – drink was the other salvation.

But we were from a born-again tradition, and if ever there is an exemplification of Weber's Protestant-Ethic-and-Spirit-of Capitalism argument, it's the Brethren movement. Education, self-improvement, inexorable upward mobility. Now the Gospel Halls are full of Mercedes-driving professionals, and they're called Evangelical Churches, or at least the ones that were classified as 'Open' Brethren are. There have been multiple splits and schisms, with Exclusive (now masquerading as the scandal-prone and thoroughly cultish 'Plymouth Brethren Christian Church') and Close Brethren still scowling away in small corners of joyless seclusion. My dad became a dentist, an RAF officer, and brought up a large and mostly well-behaved family. I am the only major disappointment.

Singing. I'd forgotten how good they are at it. Christians, that is. The Born Agains.

Oh for a thousand tongues to sing
My great Redeemer's Praise...
My grayayayayayt Redeeeeemer's praise...

I'm sitting in my unpressed travel suit, grey, my Slater's Menswear shirt-and-tie combo, rusty lungs belting it out with the rest of them, this packed Gospel Hall that isn't, not any more. It's an Evangelical Church, and trendy, interior designed, carpeted, cushioned, sleek.

The glories of my God and King
The triumphs of His Grace.

Alone, I'd be nervous, threatened, worried here, amid the saints, among the saved. The redeemed. After all, I'm a renegade, not an unbeliever but a disbeliever. They have a name for people like me, those who turned their backs on salvation, who rejected Grace, who threw away the redemption that a merciful God bestowed. Backsliders. We are backsliders. The backslidden.

I'm not alone, though. I'm surrounded by two sons complete with girlfriends, a daughter and a wife, all without exception scientifically trained atheists, all regarding this congregation of lustily bellowing believers with a kind of benign affection. Bemusement: so this is what dad has been ranting on about all this time. Behind me, my dad sits between his second wife, my stepmother, and his sister. He and my aunt are both in their 80s, both still committed to the cause of conversion, of Biblical fundamentalism. I haven't laid eyes on my aunt for a quarter of a century.

What does she see, looking at the back of my balding head? What's she thinking? Does she remember the night in 1968 when her husband, my Uncle David, was preaching at Bethany Hall, and I 'came to the Lord' at the age of 11, turning my back on the life of

22

sin and degradation and evil and sheer badness I'd lived up until that point? Reduced to hysterical tears by fear of hell and the devil and demons and the great swirling mass of black evil in the world, the evil that would sweep me up and deposit me like a piece of flotsam on hell's polluted shore?

Homer the Baptizer is a small, barrel-shaped man with wavy, iron grey hair and a crimson face that varies from clownish to thunderously holy. He is our Sunday School Superintendent at Bethany Hall, known for his bouncy way of conducting a chorus like *Store Your Treasures in the Bank of Heaven* or *Romans Ten and Nine (is a Favourite Verse of Mine)*. Tonight, though, he is in seriously adult God-conscious mode, and dressed in the strangest clothing I have ever seen in this or any gospel hall. He looks like a fisherman or a tramp, or some waterproofed combination of the two. Waders. He's wearing those thigh-high giant wellingtons river anglers use, along with oilskin leggings and jacket. But his glistening white shirt and brocade tie peeks from an opening at his neck. For some reason, a piece of string is holding this ensemble together at the waist, adding to the impression of some fallen-on-hard-times gentlemen of the road, one scared of an imminent deluge.

"Why is Mr Taylor dressed like that?" I'm whispering up into dad's Gannex shoulder. I am eight years old and this is my first baptism in our new assembly, Bethany Hall in Troon, a small town on the Ayrshire coast. The year is 1964. Harold Wilson is prime minister and his partiality for Gannex coats, made of hard, rubberised dirty-cream canvas with tartan lining, has spread to Scotland and our family. The coat smells of tyres. He's only wearing it in this overheated sweatbox of a building as we're late and standing at the back of the hall, where all kinds of unshouldered coats are hanging, some smelling stranger than dad's. Mothballs, sweat, dog, that intense whiff of urine and old jobbie some of the boys at school carry with them.

I can see what's happening at the front of the hall because we're in line with the aisle between the packed rows of folding seats. It doesn't matter for dad as he's nearly six feet (but not quite) and can see over almost any crowd in the west of Scotland, where people tend to be small. Anyway, everyone's sitting down.

Except for Homer the Baptizer, who is on the platform now, the stage, though no-one would ever call it that, where preaching is done and solos are sung. And then, suddenly, amid a vague sloshing, he begins to disappear. Down, he goes, step by step.

A large man is whispering to my dad, but I can hear him. Everyone within 20 feet can hear him. He is called Mr Godalming. Godbothering, my friend Owen calls him.

"The tank," Mr Godbothering, bellowhispers. "It's a big tank. Not like Harling Road. Or Newarthill." I understand this to be a good thing. Earlier, over high tea – not bad: three kinds of sandwich, two varieties of scone, chocolate cake and my favourite currant tart – I heard Godbothering reminiscing with my dad about Great Baptismal Accidents they had known. The shallow tank at Harling Road and the consequent concussion and hospitalization of one hapless baptismal candidate. The shortness of Newarthill's, somewhere out in the smoky steelwork wilds of Lanarkshire, which meant a particularly tall baptisee had to be sunk sitting down. "Not symbolically accurate," Godbothering had muttered.

Adult, or Believer's Baptism, not the laughable dripping or dabbing of infant's heads when they were too young to make even a slightly sensible noise, let along confess that Jesus Christ was their Lord and Saviour.

They're mostly called 'Evangelical Churches' these days, but I was brought up in a Gospel Hall, an outpost of what I knew only as 'The Brethren' or 'The Assemblies', but later came to realise was better known as 'Plymouth Brethren'. Though in fact the Scottish version of 'Brethren' was quite different in tone and social class, at least in the 1960s, from its English, Plymouth-born equivalent. In Scotland, Brethren (we were 'open', very keen to evangelise, not the very, very strict 'close' or 'closed' version) tended to flourish in fishing, mining or heavily industrialised communities. And one of the most distinctive aspects of Gospel Hall life was the open-air meeting.

If you see a street preacher nowadays, they're be-jeaned and amplified and armed with a guitar, or bellowing in a worryingly aggressive manner as embarrassed shoppers pass them by as quickly as possible. But in 1950s and '60s still-industrial Scotland, used to political and sectarian meetings and parades, and with the effects of the massive 19th century Moody and Sankey crusades still lingering, people were more used to being shouted at by a man standing on a box. And the musical accompaniment of choice was either a portable harmonium or an accordion (thought of in some Brethren circles as dangerously worldly).

I can remember shivering at the corner of Templehill and West Portland Street in Troon, watching my dad preach to nobody but the few tweedy and Homburg-hatted believers who were there for moral support. That was in the winter. In summer, both afternoon Sunday School and the evening Gospel Meeting were held on the seafront, sometimes amid massive crowds of holidaymakers. I can still feel the stifling restriction of my miniature suit, tie and polished shoes while all the other 'unsaved' bairns were in trunks or shorts, T-shirts and seemingly all holding that ultimate expression of confectionery evil, an ice cream cone from Togs, the Venice or the Beach Cafe, laden with raspberry syrup. Or, if they were posh, that unobtainable glory, the 99. With a real Cadbury's Flake.

All the Assembly children were encouraged (to be precise: bribed) to perform at these events, competing with the seagulls and the ding-dong of the ice cream vans by standing at the huge old-fashioned black microphone and singing something like *Wide, Wide as the Ocean*, or *If You don't Go To Sunday School, You'll Grow Up To Be Bad*. The man with the miniature, almost toy-sized pedal organ was there, in his brown suit. The women sat on a row of canvas chairs, all wearing more-or-less ornate hats. If you were a woman in our Gospel Hall you could neither speak nor expose your hair in public. Something to do with tempting the angels, I later learned. Who knew angels were so partial to perms and blue rinses?

Despite not being permitted to buy ice creams on a Sunday (though my dad was dangerously liberal and would even, on occasion, sneak into town late on a Sabbath evening for chips), those who sang 'at the front' were rewarded with sweeties. They were never very good sweeties. Boilings, mostly, things that came cheap in huge jars that you had to suck for hours to get any real sweetness out of. Or nasty treacle toffees. Looking back now, I realise that these were my first public performances, my first encounters with a microphone. It was the beginning of my lifelong love of ice cream in all its varieties (but especially 99s). And I hate treacle toffee to this day.

*** *** ***

So I have a hangover, caused by drinking red wine (a half-decent Co-op Rioja) and whisky (Auchentoshan 12-year-old, triple distilled but still congener-laden through the Oloroso barrels used to age it), and there's no real excuse, as it was a midweek evening and my wife doesn't drink. Why was I drinking, then? Well, it's obvious: I was obeying St Paul's advice to Timothy, about having a little wine for the stomach's sake. That's in the Bible, after all. So why are my guts giving my gyp this morning?

Earlier, I took my sore head and uneasy guts out into a stiff, Arctic wind, a morning finally beginning to taste properly of winter. It was stormy last night, the wind gusting up to violent storm 11, and while today it's almost windless, the sea is still uneasy inshore, and beyond the headlands, the swell is enormous.

Weather. Weather is more than obsession here, it's something you have to factor in to almost every major decision: will we get south this week? Will the airport at Sumburgh be closed due to fog? Will the boat sail if the winds are this bad? Should I put that scaffolding up with the forecast the way it is? Should I put to sea to check my creels or is it going to be rough as hell out by Quidawick Ness? Should I try and walk home from the dance at the local hall, or is that snow drifting deeper than I thought? And the windchill. Never, ever forget the windchill. It's always colder than it looks. Every year, cold kills people who miscalculate on windchill.

In fact, the low blink of winter sun brought one of these great moments of insight, of seeing Shetland in its wonder and glory. It's all too easy, especially befuddled on the aftermath of drink, to ignore just how beautiful this place is. You get used to the coppery red granite cliffs, the vastness of the skies, the crashing of clean, limitless water. But today I turned to look towards Gribon, home of Raymie the Poet, near where the perfectly preserved remains of a lost 18th century travellers were found buried in peat. And the headlands were smoking.

Or steaming. Great miasmas of mist enveloped them, moved in drifts through the cloudless blue sky. It took a few seconds for me to realise what I was watching. Beyond the shelter of the Faither and the Holsten, outside of the deceptive calmness of the bay, that was the Atlantic, and the rocks of Gribon were taking its full, post-storm brunt. The waves weren't so much breaking as vapourising due to the enormous force of water against rock. Spindrift, they call the effect, when a stormy sea is flattened by the power of the wind. This was different. This was like watching the sea turned into an opaque gas, by the strangest of magics. I stood, spellbound, until Ally the Postie nearly ran me down in his van. He stopped in a rattle of diesel and the screech of worn brakes.

"I've a box for Last Books," he said, the piercing on his lower lip catching the sunlight. "No papers to sign. Must be some cheapskate sending it to you."

"Ach, I'm the cheapskate, Ally," I replied. "Couldn't be bothered getting special delivery. It's just some old Ordnance Survey maps, anyway. How's the band?" Ally plays in a goth-punk industrial emo-folk outfit called Orca Bloodbath. He's from Cornwall. He is, like many soothmoothers in Shetland, reticent about his past, though it involved and still does involve rock'n'roll and all the side dishes.

"Not bad. Playing last night, but you can't have a drink if you're working next day. So it's soda water and lime all the way. No ideal for rock'n'roll at the Legion."

It's a curious fact that the notoriously conservative precincts of the British Legion in Shetland often host the most extreme local rock bands. Under a mammoth picture of the queen, the pierced and dyed cavort outlandishly.

"Good crowd?"

"Not bad. Hundred or so. No arrests, one to hospital and just the one fight. Scrotum Poles were the support. I don't think the socks-on-the-willie thing went down too well with the bar staff."

"That would be the Scrotum Poles, not you?"

"Och, no, we're too old for that kind of thing. We're fully clothed these days. Problem was, the boys in the Poles had used elastic to try and keep the socks in place – Jerry – you know Jerry – his mum had sown them in. And it was a wee bit too tight. Felix the guitarist fainted. He was the one had to be taken away to casualty. But he's fine now. Just a bit swollen."

I flinched. "Sounds like a reasonable night."

Ally reached to the passenger seat of the Royal Mail van, which was piled with packets, and handed over a sealed bundle wrapped in brown paper. My maps. Old, redundant, but good for wallpaper and nostalgia. "Better get on, Ally. See you later."

"Aye, cheers. The Scrotum Poles have a CD coming out, by the way. It's called Homus Erectile. I'll get you a copy." And with a rev and a rattle he was gone.

I reflected on the poor quality of Latin teaching, or its possible non-existence in Shetland. *Homus Erectile. Hominus erectus*, surely? I tut-tutted and shook my head like some ancient scholarly curmudgeon. *Rattus Norvegicus*, that was the name of a Stranglers album, wasn't it? I wondered if there was one in the shop? *Walking on the beaches staring at the peaches...* I tramped on, ears roaring in the icy blast of the formerly Norwegian wind.

*** *** ***

My first second hand bookshop was in Keswick, in the Lake District. Well, I say first, but for all I know my father may have carried me as a babe in arms into repositories of arcane fundamentalist tomes. In fact, he probably did.

Always, dad had huge quantities of books. Even earlier than my memory of that bookshop in Keswick (a whitewashed frontage, a house, really, not a proper shop with swirly red carpets, a basement where I felt, as an 11-year-old, somehow trapped) is the wonderful set of aromas involved in the building of new, and much needed bookshelves for our house in Glasgow. The thrilling scent of cut timber in the shop which nowadays could never be called Timberland. The grind and roar of a circular saw chopping the planks to length. The double-parking in Pollokshaws Road as the wood was stacked diagonally through the nearside front and offside rear windows of Dad's Morris Cowley. And the grunt and tear of hand-sawing, the teeth-rattling whine of an early Black and Decker power drill. I was five, and I was Dad's proud and doubtless dangerously useless helper. The dry whistle of sandpaper, the endless fuss over countersinking screws. Dad was a careful craftsman, a dental surgeon to trade and very good with his hands. Always, I have longed to be as good, with the same painstaking attention to detail. Always, things have broken, I've lost patience or just got bored. Who can forget the kitchen units keeling off a plasterboard wall, filled with dishes? Should have used bigger Rawlplugs... or the attempt to repair holes in a wall with rubber solution? Worse, the plate racks held together with carpet tacks...

Anyway, dad's bookshelves, those beautiful bookshelves, about which I can remember every detail (they were sanded, filled, painted light blue) were attached to a wall. And this was when this most exciting thing in my first seven years of life occurred. Far, far more interesting than the birth of my two sisters (apart from my attempt to electrocute one of them, but I'll leave that for the moment).

For, using his then-highly unusual power tool, dad drilled a hole in the lath and plaster wall so as to insert a Rawlplug (fibre, not plastic) which would firmly grip a retaining screw, thus stopping the bookshelves from falling on top of, well, me, a child who had already displayed a tendency to climb, pull, break, poke fingers into wall sockets, pull valve radios onto the floor by their flexes, that sort of thing. And lo, yea and forsooth, did dad not drill a hole in an unsuspected water pipe lurking inside the cavity wall? Was the water hot? Oh yes, from the back boiler of the coal fire downstairs. I remember a huge jet of steaming liquid, a graceful arc. But I was five, and small, and probably it wasn't as big as all that. For I'm certain there was a mountain in the back garden at the time, despite photographs showing it was the size of a sofa.

But I can recall my mother, dark haired, furious, looking very Irish, very Gaelic (her joint heritage – one parent from Ballymena, the other from Islay), standing there with a great wad of towel, trying to stem the water, and having to stop as it was burning her hand. There was shouting, a loud, obscure search for a plumber… great anguish, tears, and then… I can recall very little, nothing, for years afterwards.

*** *** ***

University in Glasgow in the 70s, and the old Voltaire and Rousseau bookshop at Kelvinbridge. Actually 'shop' does it an injustice; it was a mystical multi-story maze of literature, mouldering, damp, topsy turvy, higgledy piggledy, full of peculiar people, mostly scowling, many often spectacularly unkempt. And if any of this is ringing bells, you've probably read Louise Welsh's fabulous book *The Cutting Room*, one of the best portrayals of west-end Glasgow life I have ever read. She worked in Voltaire and Rousseau and captures its decaying, seductive ambience perfectly.

In 1973 I went in there and wandered, deep down, into the basements near the River Kelvin, a hideously humid place to keep books. There was no organisation as far as I could see, no classification. Everything, every discovery, was accidental, happenstance. There was Len Deighton next to Chaucer, Milton by Enid Blyton. And that's the way I like bookshops. I like the mess, or the failed organisation, with deceptive labels on shelves, a bunch of fishing tomes suddenly lurching into esoteric druggy religiosity. Which may amount to the same thing as angling, in some eyes.

*** *** ***

Here's Arnie. Arnold, Arnie to everyone. No-one less like Governor Schwarzenegger, that product of the Hitler Youth, could be imagined. Arnie is a former NATO policeman, of which there were more than a few in Shetland from the 50s onwards. The islands were, after all, on Russia's doorstep and constantly being visited by so-called spy trawlers. You can still see the remains of a NATO base nearby, perched on top of Vronnafirth Hill, the handmaiden to Hjalda, Shetland's Table Mountain. Only smaller. And less table-like. Well, maybe a coffee-table.

You drive to the top of Vronnafirth Hill, which is only about 600 feet above sea level. In these latitudes, though, every foot higher you go, it feels as if you've travelled another 100 miles north. By the time you're parking next to the radio and TV masts, you're in Arctic tundra, and you still have another 600 feet before you reach Shetland's highest point, Hjalda Hill, 1200 feet up. If Vronnafirth is rugged, a weird landscape of strange plants and wind-wiped boulders, up on the top of Hjalda Hill it's like the moon. Only windier. Strangely enough, both spots have been inhabited. The summit of Hjalda Hill sports a beautifully preserved chambered cairn, so some Picts were probably there. Dead Picts, admittedly, but to build the ornate chambers, someone must have spent a month or two amid the desolation. Vronnafirth was, until 1970, a fully-manned NATO early warning base, and technicians and NATO police were on site 24 hours a day. Admittedly, they didn't have a lot to do but play pool, put on social nights, film shows and dances, and generally enjoy themselves.

"Aye, we used to sit up there in the snow and wait for the Russians," Arnie told me. "I remember one night, we thought they'd came, one night of terrible deep snow. There was a dreadful banging on the door and someone shouting in a language we couldn't understand. But it was only Ertie from Viggabury, and some Norwegian he'd met at the Crofter's Arms. Of course, we let them in and they helped us track some bombers. Or made us drink some rum. Or maybe both. I can't recall which, exactly."

Hjalda Hill is not what you'd call a mountain. It's a rounded lump which rises, in what seems from a distance a leisurely fashion, from the lower hills around it. But as you get closer, you see the sheer red granite cliffs that rise out of the shadowed sea loch called Hjalda Voe, Shetland's longest and deepest inlet. And as you wind your way north towards the end of the Shetland mainland, North Redskerry, you realise that the road, which hugs the east coast, runs along the foot of what can only be called a massif, an uninhabited range of mini-mountains and crags with Hjalda Hill its peak.

It's a mysterious area, and one steeped in ancient history. It's remote. Radios don't work because of the rock, and neither do mobile phones. Satellite phones probably do, but the only one I know of in Shetland doesn't function. I know that because it's in a cupboard in my wife's surgery, having been given to her for use in emergencies and proved itself both incredibly expensive to run, and totally unreliable. Even if, as we tried on one occasion, you hold it right next to the Sky Plus box. The £20 set of walkie-talkies I bought off eBay has been, on the whole, more useful. Susan can go and walk the dogs and I can call her back if she gets a call.

One afternoon I was visiting a cottage, now rented out to holidaymakers, tourists and runaways, called South House with our friend Fitchen, who was doing some work for us. Fitchen, then in his 50s, was an absurdly strong man. I noticed that his watch strap had been carefully extended with nylon fishing lines, to accommodate the muscles of his wrist. We were gazing out at Da Trip, the soaring red granite cliff face opposite that rises sheer from the sea to Abram's Ward, one of Hjalda Hill's subsidiary peaks.

A gigantic cairn marks its top, and it's just the very place for sacrificing a son at God's behest or, if He is feeling beneficent, a handy lamb.

"I dinna ken about that," said Fitchen, "but I know a man who threw a dog over there."

A dog? Our host, a migration-season birdwatcher called Fran, fetched a bottle of Grouse from the cupboard and poured us both a dram. We sat in what the owners, long escaped south, call the conservatory, what the council planning department call a temporary porch, made from second-hand, indeed skip-salvaged windows and the remnants of Sullom Voe oil terminal accommodation units. The red granite of Da Trip glowed opposite us. It looked sheer, unscalable, though I knew that from the beach in front of it you could see that it sloped upward in a series of steps.

"There's a path cut o'er Da Trip," said Fitchen. "Or there used to be. It was blocked up. It's a sheep track, narrow, the rock face on one side, a sheer drop on the other. And they used to drive sheep in single file over it. It was the quickest way to get oot to da grazing at the Lang Ayre."

He sipped at the neat whisky, red-gold in reflected light.

"I was only a young man, oot helping with caaing of the sheep. And the dogs, the dogs weren't used to the height. One of them just froze on the path. So Ertie o'da Lums, old Ertie, no' here now, he was shouting and bawling at the dog, trying to get it to move. But it wouldna. It just stood there, that way a dog does, back legs shaking, couldna move back or forward."

I tried to imagine the fear in that animal. Shetland sheepdogs are some of the most intelligent, energetic, physically adept canines on earth. Too intelligent by half. They're almost useless as pets as they need to be worked to keep their brains occupied. As pets they will gnaw through partition walls, jump into your arms from a distance of seven feet, fight with every other dog that comes their way and kill the sheep they were never taught to round up. They can also see (in black and white, apparently) in incredible detail and enormous distances.

We briefly owned a Shetland sheep dog called Yum Yum (something to do with the Teletubbies, I think) who could only be contained in a special concrete block outhouse which had been lined with sheets of steel. He was put down after he casually killed seven of a neighbour's prize Suffolk crosses. For fun. He was bored.

"So in the end," said Fitchen, "Ertie just walks up to the dog, picks him up and throws him over the edge. Didna make a sound as he fell. Hundred feet or so, right down to the shingle beach." Fitchen gave a melancholy smile. "Worst of it was, the dog got up and limped away. Limped into the sea and just… disappeared. Ertie and me just stood looking down, looking at where it had gone into the water, and then Ertie says, "Bastarding dug. He was just fed three days ago.""

*** *** ***

33

Yum Yum was preceded by the nicest dog in the world, Quoyle the Labrador, bought from a litter over on the west side of Shetland, in the Bohemian Enclave, where drug-smoking children run wild and hippies cavort naked on a May morn. He's no longer with us, ending his days doddery and incontinent at 14, growing moment by moment much less pleasant in nature, too. He was, if it's true that dogs age seven times faster than humans, 98, so I suppose I have to be kind. But towards the end he was still capable of ripping bins apart in search of tasty titbits, sneaking off under cover of darkness to try and scavenge treats from neighbours, and happy to swim in the sea for hours before rolling in anything dead and smelly he could find. I'm not sure that age withered him properly. Eventually, I took him outside, fed him his favourite cheese and we parted company. It was the traditional way to deal with dogs, I'd been told. I buried him in the garden, next to the oil tank.

I gave the shotgun back. I've never fired a weapon since.

Lulu, our current dog, is a smooth-coated St Bernard, 12 stones of somnambulance for 98 per cent of the time. However, when she rouses herself, normally because her gigantic nose is telling her that bacon is frying or that somewhere within an area of 20 square miles there's a barbecue planned, she can become frisky. And when 12 stones of canine is in play mode, beware. One swoosh of that massive tail can decimate a table of glassware. She once broke two of my ribs. By accident. She is, without a doubt, the best-natured and gentlest dog I have ever come across. A neighbour's tiny three-year-old daughter had undergone a horrible nipping experience with one of those pesky mini-dogs and was fearful of all breeds, before she met Lulu. Who, when faced with human creatures smaller than her (and many, if not most, are) tends to behave in the most restrained, careful manner imaginable.

At first Leila wouldn't come into the house. It took a prolonged session of Lulu-encounter therapy, during which large quantities of disgusting St Bernard slobber was dripped, and she was encouraged to poke the big beast in the jowls, pull her ears and engage in other such actions considered signs of affection in Bernardland, to establish a relationship. Since then they have been the fastest and funniest of friends.

The problem with Lulu is her tendency to lean. This is a St Bernardine trait, and relates to their usefulness as rescue dogs in the snow-bound fastnesses of the Alps. It seems that when they nose out a lost climber or skier, they burrow in beside them and use their ample bodies to warm up their companion. In Lulu, this results in her silently approaching unsuspecting strangers, sitting down beside them, and then allowing her entire weight to fall on their legs. Toppling can and does result.

Immensely territorial, craving human companionship, loyal and just… big. That's St Bernards. We did have two. The runt of the same litter Lulu came from was adopted just before she could be sent for termination, her show potential destroyed by a faulty eye. Lucy, she was called. She did not live long. And when she died, of cancer, her absence was very hard to cope with, for us and for Lulu, who was in mourning for a month. The sheer physical size and personality of these dogs means they fill large spaces in your life. Taking Lucy to the vet for her final journey, emaciated and yet still enormous, was a dreadful experience. A shotgun would have been unthinkable.

Quoyle doesn't haunt my dreams. Killing is a part of crofting, and when you live in a community like this, you inevitably participate. Sheep, pigs even cows, goats, ducks, hens, geese. Shooting, bleeding, butchering. Eating. A friend used to be a postman in his youth, and one of the expected duties of the postie (no longer) was to collect unwanted kittens (kitlings) from houses on his round, and drown them.

He didn't eat them, though.

Aurora

I want to tell you about the Northern Lights. I sit with the witnesses, the narrators, the diarists and describers, from Aristotle through George Low, Minister of Birsay and Harry in Orkney between 1774 and 1795, right up to the bloggers and photographers of today, swamping social media with their symphonies in white and green, always green, great wiggly waves across a midnight blue sky.

But it's not like that. The aurora borealis, captured on absurdly long exposures by frostbitten snappers on folding chairs, makes for a beautiful picture, but not an accurate one. But then, neither does a more realistic photo showing a strange, if one-dimensional glow. Green again. That's the oxygen, struck by electrified particles from the sun. The further north the greener. The reds – from nitrogen – tends to be seen in more southerly climes.

Because the Northern Lights, Da Mirrie Dancers in Shetlandic, move, flicker, sprint across the sky, beam imperiously like some Nuremberg rally, and occasionally envelope you in a sense of otherness, of alien interference. Buzzing. Sometimes there's an odd rattle and hum, and not just from that U2 album you left playing in the car. Orcadians have been known to compare this to the rustling of silk, while the Lapps say, beautifully, that it's similar to the cracking of reindeer leg joints as they run.

Aristotle, in his *Meteorologica*, managed to catch the lights as far south as Greece, comparing them to jumping goats. The names, the words are always quaint, often lovely. Galileo, also far to the south, named the phenomenon *Boreale Aurora* – northern dawn. The Finns call it *revontulet*, foxfire, because they thought, or a poet told them to think, that the lights were caused by sparks from the coat of the Arctic Fox. *Nordlys* may be an obvious Danish translation, but in the folklore of Denmark, it is swans flapping their wings while they try to free themselves from the ice they're trapped in.

The Umingmaktormuit Inuit – known as the Musk-ox People – had shamen who believed they could control the lights through whistling and spitting, while some Sami thought the aurora posed a threat. Bare-headed, you risked burning, and it could become 'entangled in the hair'. Everyone tried to stay silent while the lights were active.

What else could the lights be? Ancients racked their imaginations and blamed the glinting of shoals of herring, the reflections of fires or shards of ice in the sky.

But as we now know, it's sunspots. Or solar winds. Of course it is. Whatever those are…

There are various scientific websites which predict, more or less accurately, electro-magnetic activity and will send you alerts by Twitter or email. In Shetland, these periods of massive sunspot action often coincide with heavy cloud. I once met an excited tourist, heading north into the social withdrawal which can be Shetland at New Year. I was in a shared cabin on the ferry, snoring badly enough to wake the undead, and certainly enough to keep this poor soul from Kettering awake and divorced from his dreams. He was heading up to Shetland for the weekend, he said, to see the Northern Lights. Really, I said, in the wakefulness between snores. Where was he staying? Lerwick, came the reply. Did he plan to hire a car, get out and about? No.

As it happens, there was little auroral activity that weekend, and low cloud anyway. Lerwick, with its street lights and traffic, swamps faint auroras in visual pollution, but sometimes, sometimes it falls prey to the natural phenomenon of the Dancers in a splendid and spectacular way. I'll never forget one Up Helly Aa, in the early 1990s, with all the town's street lights switched off for the procession, when the aurora burst forth in its full majesty. And as the 'vikings' and other guizers paraded, shouted, set fire to the galley, there were inescapable thoughts of Norse traditions that the lights were a bridge to Valhalla, that they signified a journey to another world.

It's easy to make mistakes. Many visitors have left Shetland convinced that the orange flares from the Sullom Voe Oil Terminal and gas plant, lurking below the horizon, are the aurora.

But there's a difference. When you see the Lights in their full, naked glory, it can leave you disturbed, haunted. Spellbound.

For me they will always be associated with the taste of Jameson's Irish whiskey, as the first time I witnessed Da Mirrie Dancers, I was in glittering, ice cold frost outside my then girlfriend's house in Voe, that crossroads village at the Shetland Mainland's centre, where roads lead north, south, east and west.

I was a mere visitor then, in the process of falling in love. With a person, a place, a people. We had just returned from an extraordinary meal at Burrastow House on the far west side of Shetland, where in those days proprietor Harry Tuckey would serve you candlelit winter dinners of pearl-peppered mussels and freshly shot hare, great old Rioja, home-made bread, all in oak-panelled rooms smelling of polish and peat. We returned home replete, driving carefully on ungritted roads into the swirling sky.

The stars swam in great shifting sheets of ice, as swans flapped their wings, herring flew, and warriors flexed their armour as they travelled to eternity. Foxes shook their hair, sending crystals of pure light towards us. I staggered in delight around the garden, bottle in hand, then grew solemn. Where was I? What was happening to me?

Shetland was.

One trillion watts, they reckon, passing through the sky, passing through me. One million amps. Louder than bombs, louder than Led Zeppelin. Louder than my heart.

Now, here in The Last Bookshop, sitting at a desk in this ancient manse, I read the Rev Low and wonder about the minister of that time here in Quidawick. Did he welcome George to his home? This is the house where over hundreds of years a succession of clerics interviewed the doubting, the desperate and the damned, and contemplated creation. Where one of them condemned Katherine Jonesdochter, the last Shetland 'witch' to be executed, horribly killed in a barrel of boiling tar.

I prefer George Low, with his clear scientific passion. In fact it was beyond passion. Let me tell you about Rev Low, naturalist, author, first real Shetland islands tourist, Kirk minister, maker and user of microscopes to the extent that he blinded himself. He wrote *Fauna Orcadensis; or, The natural history of the quadrupeds, birds, reptiles and fishes of Orkney and Shetland*. But it remained unpublished until long after his death, and the accompanying *Flora Orcadensis* has vanished. His extensive and careful writings were widely distributed to his contacts among the antiquarians and natural historians of Scotland, but, to put it bluntly, he was ripped off and exploited by those who considered themselves his betters. In his *A Tour through the islands of Orkney and Shetland, Containing hints relative to their ancient, modern, and natural history*, collected in 1774, he writes this about his time in the darkness of Orcadian winters:

> '*Meteors are frequent, but as yet we are not so familiarised to them, as to those the Philosophers cal the Aurora Borealis or northern lights, and by our country sages, on account of their motion The Merry Dancers, which are the constant attendants of our clearer evenings, and much relieve the gloom of our long winter nights.*'

He was born in Edzell, Angus, in 1747, and educated at Marischal College, Aberdeen, and then St Andrews University. In 1768, George went to Stromness as a tutor, and that was the beginning of his obsessive study of Orkney, Shetland, of the birds, flora and fauna, and marine life in and around the northern isles. He built his own microscope. Did he grind the lenses, solder the casings? In 1771, George was licensed as a Minister by the Presbytery of Cairston, but stayed in Stromness. In 1774 he began the tour of Orkney and Shetland which would lead to his book. A book which provided, among other things, the first real engagement in literature with Shetland dialect, including the Lord's Prayer in ancient Norn. And he was installed as minister at Birsay and

Harray, where he was 'greatly beloved by his flock'. He married a fellow local minister's daughter, but his wife died in 1776 after giving birth to a dead child. Reading between the lines of his entry in the Dictionary of National Biography, with its use of terms like 'unfortunate', 'futile', 'scant recognition' and 'bitterness', he sank into frustration and depression.

According to his biography at the University of Edinburgh Archives, 'Extensive use of the microscope during his research probably contributed to the onset of opthalmia and near complete blindness by 1793, thus cutting him off from his studies. George Low died in Orkney on 13 March 1795.' Aged just 49.

I think of George Low, his eyesight fading to black, outside at Birsay, straining and failing to see anything as he gazed sightlessly at the skies, as the aurora crackled around him like the rustling of a dancing woman's dress. His mood, black as blindness as Da Mirrie Dancers frolicked around him. And I think of him here, in Quidawick, as I gaze out of the manse – the bookshop – window. Because he would have come here, to this ancient, important in the 1770s, building, though not to this room, which was added a few years later. The aurora may have shone for him here, as it did upon him even while his own inner darkness increased and his eyesight dimmed.

He's buried beneath the pulpit at the kirk in Birsay, presumably St Magnus' Kirk, built on the ancient Christ Church, where Earl Magnus himself was brought after being murdered, martyred on Egilsay.

Oh, George. Martyred to an intellect that was unappreciated by your generation. Blinded as the aurora danced, merrily above you. Crushed by the death of wife and child, the snobbish exploitation of others. Eight volumes, your *Tour of Orkney and Shetland* is. Unpublished until 84 years after your death. Now recognised as utterly crucial to the study of this place, its language, its people, its life. It's in museums, archives, libraries. But I don't have it here in The Last Bookshop. I wish I did.

Afloat

Here's a book for you. Get it on Amazon for 0.01 British pounds if you must, but remember you'll pay almost three quid for postage and the author will get nothing. Honestly, second hand books! It's a disgusting exploitation of content with no benefit to the copyright owner. If you must buy used, then put yourself through the guilt-trip to Shetland, come to The Last Bookshop and give me your money. Because I deserve it. Or even if I don't, it'll make you feel better.

Anyway, paperback for a penny if you insist on sailing down The Big Scummy River of Literary Evil (where I not so secretly source some of my, ah, stock, like every bookshop in the world. And don't even mention the couthy coffee-shop repositories of self-righteous bookshopdom that simply nip round to Tesco or Asda for their discounted hardback pulp, then flog them to 'loyal customers' at full price...)

Ahem. I'm not talking about *Shetland, Sailing directions and Anchorages* (worthy, if out of date in the edition I have). I'm talking about *Coasting*, by Jonathan Raban. Not just the modern British masterpiece of seafaring, but a brilliant evocation of what it meant to be British, or English, at the time of the Falklands War. An exploration of Scotland, England and the Isle of Man. And a superbly poignant memoir to boot.

I love this book. I've read it many times, bought several copies for friends. Like the author's other works energised by a state of flotation (*Old Glory, Voyage to Juneau, Foreign Land, Hunting Mr Heartbreak*, all excellent) they not only capture all the threat, joy and terror of sailing, inshore and deep sea, but they use the ship, yacht or dinghy as a means of transport to beauty, memory and truth.

And his love of the sea, of boats – he can no longer sail, these days, after being confined to a Seattle wheelchair by a stroke – resonates not just with thousands of armchair navigators but with me in particular, I think, because I have chosen this strange life of semi-buoyancy aboard Shetland. This lump of land is my vessel now. It wasn't always the case. For I have had a love affair with floating things that goes back to childhood bathtimes.

Actually, that was initially a fascination with not above-the-waves ships but, submarines. Those wee subs you used to get free with breakfast cereal that you added a dab of bicarb to, and which would dive and then resurface as the powder dissolved. Fuelled by a later reading, at a highly impressionable age, of that classic of nuclear submarine propaganda, *Nautilus 90 North*, then incessant viewings of submarine movies, culminating in days, weeks of immersion in Wolfgang Peterson's superb *Das Boot*, in German of course. These days I peer through binoculars from my son's house in Innellan on the Clyde at the massive, sullen shapes of Trident-deliverers shouldering out to sea or heading back to port at Faslane. And I can't help it. I feel a dark thrill. On my personal bucket list remain four trips – to the chopped-in-half U-Boat, U-534, you can visit in Birkenhead, the still-intact boats at Keil and Bremerhaven, and the one at the Chicago Museum of Science and Technology. Dive, dive, dive…

Boyhood rowing trips off Largs, and the occasional late night expedition on one of the larger wooden fishing boats operating off what was essentially Glasgow's stony beach, would occasionally bring one of the then-Polaris subs within breathtaking range, as we wallowed halfway to Cumbrae. Fortunately, there was never an actual confrontation with one. I mean, who would have blinked first?

There were visits to Glasgow's boating ponds, a dreadful incident in Maxwell Park, where a much-prized clockwork model launch sank into the muddy depths. I recall my mother having the pond drained, but surely I must be imagining that? The launch was returned, rusted and clogged with black filth. Other ponds in

Glasgow hosted serious model makers' outings, with huge scale models of warships which possessed working smokestacks and even working guns. Compared to them my ham-fisted Airfix models of Warspite and HMS *Hood* were paltry, glue-festooned things. Too complex for an eternally impatient youth to assemble effectively.

Two decades later, I would walk into a living room in Burnside, quaking, to meet Jack, who had only survived the *Bismarck*'s sinking of the *Hood* through being invalided off the ship before its last voyage, by dint of his appallingly infected feet (the Royal Navy never had boots big enough for him). Jack's daughter Susan was pregnant, and I was responsible. We were planning to get married, and it was generally considered a good idea for me to meet my impending parents-in-law. Jack, a charming man who in fact didn't have long to live, look sternly at me, took my hand and asked: "Will a shotgun be necessary?"

Aged seven, I was moved from the south side of Glasgow to Troon, which had its own beaches, though I never felt they had the raffish fish and chip glamour of Largs, away to the north. My father decided to take up sailing, and acquired an ancient Enterprise sailing dinghy, which he insisted I should crew for him every summer Saturday afternoon. On the cusp of adolescence, I hated this. Especially when one ill-advised trip out in a gale saw us capsized and swept onto the breaker's yard breakwater of Troon Harbour, to be rescued by the yachting club bores, their hilarity ill-disguised, in their stand-by motorboat. These bourgeois boatiefolk in their GP14s and Shearwater catamarans saw dad and me as lumbering idiots who would never appear on Sundays for racing, due to our uncompromisingly land-based Sabbatarianism. As we dried ourselves off and desperately tried to warm up, I remember hearing one loudmouth braying through in the yachting club bar: "I've seen some strange things washed up on the breakwater, but that's the first time a yellow Enterprise has ended up there!"

The shame gripped tighter and more chilling than any hypothermia could. I never went sailing with my father again, finding endless excuses, alternative Saturday pursuits such as the rugby I hated and was incompetent at, but which was at least away from family, gospel hall and the patronising stench of yachtiness.

Five years ago I bought my own yellow Enterprise, with the ill-conceived notion of learning, or relearning the sailing skills necessary to parade around St Magnus' Bay. It was an eBay purchase, towed by the Perthshire seller, who probably couldn't believe his luck, to the ferry in Aberdeen. This dinghy was fibreglass, when my dad's had been plywood, and was a horribly frisky adornment to the little bay in front of The Last Bookshop for, oh, a month. Far from confronting and defusing ancient memories and fears, that horrid little boat simply inflamed them. I'd paddle out to her in an inflatable (I'd called her *Geni*, just like that far-off monstrous Ayrshire dinghy) climb in and think... I can't be bothered with this. All the guddle of ropes and sails, or worse, the hideously unreliable motor, a vintage British Seagull. So I'd sit for a bit, floating, and then climb back into the my rubber life preserver and paddle slowly back to shore.

"Been sailing?" my wife would ask.

"Yes," I'd reply.

*** *** ***

Another book, or rather series of books. I can hardly bring myself to mention the three words that instantly set off in me a whole ship's complement of emotions: regret, that, as I recognise now, I'll never own a sea-going boat you can voyage in, sleep in, travel in, have adventures in. Fear, as I remember the occasionally terrifying 'adventures' I have had at sea. And that secret relief and joy that, in the end, you can live things through books that you don't have to do in real life.

Swallows and Amazons. I don't have to spend every Easter or summer on Lake Windermere (though I remember a few family holidays there with affections). *We Didn't Mean To Go To Sea*. I don't have to sail in canal or a river, for which I have an odd, never rationalised aversion. *Winter Holiday*, my favourite of Arthur Ransome's books, to be consumed, guiltily, just before Christmas every year, thrilling and shivering to the stories of an ice-bound lake, a trek through the snow, and eventual deliverance.

Winter Holiday is almost certainly an allegory for Ransome's own, very real adventures in escaping from Russia, in the company of Trotsky's secretary, Evgenia Petrovna Shelepina, immediately after the Revolution. He was either a blundering idiot or a very clever British spy, but one way or another he made his way to Britain, married Evgenia, and any remaining thrillseeking was channelled into messing about in boats and then writing about them. The fact that he had to write about children and their relationship with waters deep and shallow seems to have left him in a state of rancour and general moustachioed grumpiness for most of his life.

Great Northern? is as close as the various sweet Swallows and grumpy Amazons ever came to Shetland, but they never landed here. There is a hint of what Ransome might have done with them in the pre-World War Two novel *The Shetland Plan*, by prolific ex-naval officer and oceanic writer 'Taffrail' (Henry Taprell Dorling), who was stationed here during World War One. I love this book, because there's a joy in trying to piece together the travels of its protagonists through the isles. Real places, uncluttered by the press of modernity, and lightly fictionalised. And I suppose this is the time to mention Miss Anne of Cleeves, and her Jimmy Perez crime books, later made into a successful and long-running TV series.

"But... but... you can't get there from there!" There was a degree of spluttering from Shetlanders at some of the geographical liberties taken by the makers of *Shetland* the TV series, where characters were forever walking from Karaness to Sumburgh in seconds, wandering that lonely mountainside next to the Gilbert Bain Hospital, or squelching through the wild moorland just behind Commercial Street in Lerwick.

It all looked moodily beautiful, of course, and if you haven't been to Shetland, the fact that in reality it's a 35-minute drive from Lerwick to Quidawick, not a 10-second stroll, matters not a whit. It's the telly, after all.

In print, too, liberties with landscape are often taken by writers who want to employ a particular setting but avoid going into too much detail. Sometimes there are good reasons for that. After all, you don't want to libel the inhabitant of a particular, identifiable house as a murdering psychopath, do you? Though you will be able to find The Last Bookshop from the description in this book, of course. Otherwise, how would I do any business?

And yet there is delight for readers in being able to inhabit the genuine version of a fictional world. Anne Cleeves has recognised this with her non-fiction book Anne Cleeves' Shetland and the "book locations" map on her website. Fascinating hours can be spent following in Jimmy Perez's footsteps. It's fun, and you don't have to murder anyone. Unless you really want to.

There are other Shetland-set books offering the possibility of literary tourism, from probably the greatest Shetland novel – Robert Allan Jamieson's *Thin Wealth* – to the riotous brilliance of Frank Renwick's Unst and Yell epic *Noost*. But my favourite is long out of print, although it was an enormous success when it was first published 77 years ago. Available from me, of course, but sporadically as I have to seek out old copies. That would be £15 for a rough old no-dustjacket reading copy and £60 in good condition. Sorry about that. Well, not really.

Henry Taprell Dorling, who was a prolific writer of fiction under the pen name Taffrail, was born in 1883 and had a career as an officer in the Royal Navy which spanned both First and Second World Wars. His first book, *Pincher Martin*, is probably his best known, but he published dozens of enormously successful novels during a long life which ended in 1968. And in 1939 he published *The Shetland Plan*.

Angus in the Shetland Archives found Dorling's obituary in *The Times*, which only hints at what was a very colourful Naval career, from The Relief of Peking (Beijing) in 1900 through North Sea destroyer and mine layer action in World War One to staff work for the Commander in Chief (Mediterranean) during World War Two. There is no biographical detail about his time in Shetland, but it's clear from *The Shetland Plan* that he spent enough time in the isles, probably during World War One, to amass a great deal of detailed local knowledge.

During World War One, Swarbacks Minn, the deep, sheltered channel bounded by the islands of Muckle Roe, Papa Little and Vementry, was the base for the Royal Navy's 10th Cruiser Squadron – something celebrated last year by the Voe Bakery, which was founded in 1915 specifically to supply the fleet with bread, pies and cakes. You can still see the 10-inch guns which were mounted on Vementry to defend the ships. *The Shetland Plan* is largely set, both at sea and land, in an area stretching from Papa Stour to Bridge of Walls and on to Voe, with trips to Brae, Lerwick, Scalloway and the mysterious and very isolated house called Jackville at Binna Ness (sold in 2015 and currently being renovated).

Although published after World War Two had started, *The Shetland Plan* was written in 1937 and 1938, and its plot must have seemed terrifyingly plausible to readers 77 years ago. An author's note from September 1939 stresses that "this novel was in its proof stage before the outbreak of the present war. Needless to say, the events described exist only in my imagination." But a German plan to land spies, arms and explosive in Shetland by submarine in the run-up to what Taffrail certainly saw in 1937 as an inevitable war must have at least been considered in Berlin and anticipated in London. Hence the massive build up of troops and defences in the isles almost as soon as war was declared.

The book itself has, initially, an extremely Ransomely feel – and is full of a jaunty, upper middle class, jolly-hockey-sticks sense of well-heeled Englishness. The Rivers family (retired Naval officer Andy, teenage son John, 20-something daughter Margaret, a wife referred to only as Mrs (!) Rivers and a dog, Sandy, who is always vomiting) come to Shetland in August for a fishing holiday.

Every stage of their trip north is beautifully described – half the family travel by air from Aberdeen, half take their car aboard the fictional ship *Scalloway Princess*. But it's when they arrive in Shetland that Dorling, with some clear help from the Ordnance Survey, gets down to detail and conjures up what travel in the isles was like nearly eight decades ago.

The road twisted and turned through many right angles, sometimes almost doubling on its tracks. They passed over a little bridge, with the Loch of Strom to the right, and Stromness Voe to the left – through the cluster of houses called Olligarth, and along the east side of the inlet called Weisdale Voe. A sharp turn at the head of it found them climbing a long slope, with the road cut out of the hillside and the voe, with its green foreshore and a little village with a few scattered dwellings, far below. Then, right between the Hill of Sound and Leaskie Knowe, over the Burn of Tactigill and so downhill through the villages of Tresta and Bixter, with views of Tresta Voe, the Firth, the Ness of Bixter and Effirth Voes on the left...

This description, complete with odd spellings, is early in the novel and prepares you for a glorious set of drives, walks and sea voyages on and around the isles. The family meet a mysterious German refugee called Mr Boomer, the landowner Sir Richard Carmel and his wife, Lady Carmel (who also has a repulsive dog), and their daughter Alice. The Carmels have a 50-foot motor boat called *Olna* which is crucial to the action. This involves the sighting of a submarine, the discovery of an arms cache at the abandoned whaling station also called Olna (between Voe and Brae), and the pursuit of a gang of German spies who murder one of the main characters (Mr Boomer, actually, who turns out to be a bit of a hero). An aircraft carrier, several destroyers and a survey ship are involved. While the book begins in quite a jokey, *Swallows and Amazons* sort of way, it ends with major bloodshed, explosions, death and destruction. There is, as you might expect, frequent rampant sexism and gender stereotyping, not to mention some rough attempts at Shetland dialect and misspelled place names. But it has tremendous pace and, as I say, a delight in and sense of place.

I spent a day tracing the locations mentioned in the book and travelling to them by car. I would love, in summer, to follow the *Olna*'s marine voyages, especially the high speed trip to Scalloway and back to Bridge of Walls and then Gonfirth and Voe. I was especially interested in the family's base while in Shetland, "The Bridge of Walls Hotel". After a bit of research, or asking folk in the pub, I discovered that the long, extended straggle of old houses just opposite the bus stop at Brig o' Waas had indeed been a former shop and fishing hotel, at a time when angling in Shetland and Orkney was a major tourism attraction. I'd never even given the place, now a private house, a second glance, but sure enough, the description in *The Shetland Plan* still matches up:

> *The hotel obviously hadn't been built as such. It looked more like three cottages knocked into one – a long, two storied house of grey stone, with a row of dormer windows in the slate roof giving light and air to the bedrooms on the second floor. It stood on a terrace overlooking a narrow patch of walled garden, beyond which was Browland Voe.*

I had more trouble with Sir Richard and Lady Carmel's house "near a little village called Gonfirth" reached in the Carmels' chauffeur-driven Mostyn car by driving...

> *... to the little village of Aith and, twisting and turning, along part of the east shore of Aith Voe, through East Burrafirth, up hill and down again over a tract of wild, undulating moorland, and so to Gonfirth. From here, turning left, the chauffeur came down to low gear to negotiate what was little more than a rough cart track winding through the heather, with view of sea and islands in the distance.*

I initially thought Dorling was describing East House, Grobsness, though South Voxter and the abandoned Lea of Gonfirth were also possibilities. However, the fact that "Andy recognised the old anchorage of the Tenth Cruiser Squadron... the irreverent used to call them The Muckle Flugga Hussars" also made me think of the Old Haa at Grobsness. It's a lot of fun to speculate and a tramp about may give you some ideas. Bearing in mind the decades since it was written, much could have changed. But some things haven't:

It was a row of three or four squat, single-storeyed cottages apparently knocked into one, with some modern looking outbuildings at the far end. They lay within 50 yards of the rock shore of Gonfirth, with a stretch of sloping lawn...

The 'big hoose' at Vementry, still beautifully maintained by its largely absent owners, fits the description exactly and has a holiday cottage nearby you can rent if you so desire.

The "derelict whaling station" at Olna still looks very much like a derelict whaling station, its pier littered with scrap. Voe, one of the most beautiful villages in Shetland, still has its bakery, though the shop referred to in *The Shetland Plan* is now the Pierhead Bar and Restaurant. Souther Hill, crucial to the plot and site of one of the most gruesome scenes (though Dorling only hints that a body is found with ravens having pecked out its eyes) is probably best viewed from the steep, almost alpine road to The Lost Valley of Collafirth.

And then there's the story's finale, which takes place in two locations I think deliberately made vague, as one is the home of a gang of treacherous spies and is, in fact, blown off the face of the earth, while the other is the crofthouse of their local collaborator, who shops "in a certain village about seven miles away" from Bridge of Walls.

This is either Voe, Aith or Bixter (with some liberties taken in terms of distance) and as the croft can only be reached by "several miles of trekking over rough ground" with cup-like depressions in the ground and small hummocky hills on the way, my money is on the still rather mysterious community of Tumblin, where the road runs out and you can indeed hike over the hills to Voe or Aith. If you're feeling adventurous and have a stout pair of hobnailed boots, the right sort of mackintosh (the coat, not the computer) and a deerstalker hat. Jolly good!

The Shetland Plan always transports me to a different Shetland. One where tweedy, wealthy families rejoiced in 'plain mutton teas' and roaring fires, despised mackerel fishing as far too easy and effortlessly patronised the 'characterful' Shetlanders. And of course you had to bring your own gin and whisky as the islands were entirely dry, with neither pub nor off licence. All of which may seem alienating. But the book actually provides a sense of wonderment, of joy, in a landscape which, as you retrace the Rivers family's increasingly scary steps, remains very much as it was on the eve of war. As for the weather, some things never change...

It blew like the wrath of God – a roaring, tearing, rampaging gale which flattened growing crops and shrieked through the tough heather. The water from the voes was hidden by a layer of wind-flung spume like dense white smoke. Every little burn was in spate, bursting with miniature waterfalls and rapids. Each loch was a small, wildly agitated ocean stained almost to the colour of deep mahogany, with its lee shore, and the weather faces of its islets, fringed with foam like whipped cream or soapsuds...

*** *** ***

A quite wise, or at least relatively clever, man said to me, a few weeks after my arrival in the isles from points sooth a quarter-century ago, that I would have to decide where I stood on boats. Not, as it were, making sure I kept my feet amidships so as not to cause a capsize, but whether or not I was truly, madly deeply 'boatie'.

"In Shetland," he said "people are either massively boatie, or else they hate them with a great hatred and avoid them at all costs."

I have since found this to be an overstatement, but with a grain of truth in it that pertains not just to

Shetland but to other island communities too. In a place where boats are essential to so many people's

livelihoods, not to mention for the transportation of goods and folk back and forward both within the archipelago and to The Land of Scots, you can fall in love with the sea and floating about on it. Or you can learn to hate it for the damage and discomfort it causes. You can put yourself into a state of denial, and pretend you live in, oh, I don't know, Crieff, ostensibly the furthest point from the sea in Scotland. But it's not easy.

When I arrived in Shetland I immediately became obsessed with getting out to sea. This was, for me, provoked by its proximity. Water was everywhere, and there were all those voes and geos, nooks and crannies inviting exploration. Not mention the idea of catching fish. All this in an environment where sewage, if it existed at all, was quickly sent along the mysterious pipeline to Orkney.

My girlfriend had a tiny Mirror dinghy, we were living in the picture postcard fjord village of Voe, and having acquired an ancient two-stroke, clutchless Clinton motor, the kind known as 'make or break', I spent a few weeks pottering about between there and Brae. And I discovered that wondrous feeling of escape, of shedding all the troubles of the day, as you cast off and just... floated.

So I began looking for something bigger, something proper, and it's a search that continues to this day. It began with the aforementioned Wise Man of the Central Mainland and I examining a plywood yacht in Burra. "The first thing you need when looking at wooden boat," said The Wise Man, "is a penknife. You need to see what condition the wood is in." Whereupon he buried the knife, way past the hilt, into the transom, which was wet, rotting and apparently made out of sodden paper maché. I didn't buy it.

I did, however, buy – let's see – four Shetland Models, the double-ended open boat based on traditional Norse designs. The first was Kenny Johnson's old school project, made in titanically heavy glassfibre, which had been lying on the beach at Vidlin for a decade. It needed new rubbing strips and a coat of paint, and about ten strong men and women to slide it, grumbling, into the water. The trusty Clinton motor on the stern quarter just about made it go, and it went with us to Cromarty in the Black Isle, where I imagine it languishes still, taking tourists out to annoy dolphins.

The second Model, *Fram*, was around 21 foot long, about 60 years old, or at least half of it was. The top half of the hull was plywood (blasphemy!), and it had its original (probably) Stuart-Turner engine, started with either a massive handle or a sulky, home-made electric bodge. I say 'started'. Sometimes it did, sometimes it didn't. I had it for two years, two years of repairs, collision with piers, and the perennial bailing-until-it-stops-leaking business after you put it in the water for the first time. It would take around three weeks for the lower planks to expand and stop the thing leaking. Thank goodness for the wave pump. I think it's still in or outside a shed in Ramnavine. I still get nightmares about trying to restart that engine off the Faither.

Then there was a really rather good dark green fibreglass Model that, for once, was light and quite easy to launch. Too light, actually. It was downright frisky, breaking its moorings in a gale (Alyn and I chased it down in a salmon workboat as it disappeared towards the Atlantic. I just managed to get aboard and the four-stroke Japanese outboard started at the first pull). After that came a couple of small dinghies, both really too wee to be safe. Though that didn't stop one of them being borrowed by a couple of professional mountaineers who were working for Shetland Amenity Trust on a project to count rare plants growing on the cliffs of Hjalda Voe. The shear pin failed on the motor during a gale and only their amazing fitness got them home safely, thanks to a two-hour frenzy of paddling from the Lang Ayre to Heylor.

Two years ago I bought a lovely Shetland Model with a cabin, rigged for sailing, and along with it rented a berth at the Brae Marina. There followed two years of pumping, bailing, battery charging, repairs to storm damage and general boatie activity up to and not including actually going out to sea in her. Never has the definition of a boat as "a hole in the water you throw money into" seemed more appropriate. The longest trip I made on her was when I took her from the berth to the marina pier, having sold her to Franz Culliman from Thule. He trailered her to East Almafirth and then she was towed behind the *Westering (*why not *Eastering?)* to her presumably new (and presumably eternal) home.

To be honest, the vessels that have lasted longest in my ownership and have provided the most consistent fun, fish and flotation have been two plastic sit-on-top kayaks (I've tried the 'proper' kind where you deliberately trap your legs in a tube, and hated them with a great and abiding hatred) and a wee rubber HonWave dinghy with a four-stroke Japanese engine. They sit outside all year round, require no maintenance to speak of (the engine is purged and cleaned and kept indoors over the winter) and can be used at a moment's notice. Using the kayaks, we have explored the caves of the Quidawick Ness, and the wee HonWave has caught its weight in mackerel many times over.

The berth in Brae has just gone, passed on to a neighbour who has a sizeable boat and knows how to use it. My *Swallows and Amazons* dreams of overnight voyages to Norway or, at a pinch, Aith have been shelved. But as the weather continues to improve, the kayaks and the wee rubber dinghy await. Being boatie in Shetland isn't something you give up easily.

***   ***   ***

One last word about Raban's *Coasting*: there is a memorable chapter in the book where the author meets a fellow liveaboard vagabond, someone called Nick who has given up his shoreside life to sail his tiny fibreglass sloop *Sussex Rowan* along the coast of England, full of dreams of maybe heading to Africa. Nick is an appealing figure, scraping by on social security, gradually building the sea-skills needed to pursue his deep-sea ambitions.

I was curious as to what may have befallen Nick since *Coasting* was published in 1985. An internet search brought up an article in the September 1998 edition of the American magazine *Cruising World*. It told of an episode in the strange and sinister history of Palmyra, the so-called 'cursed' Pacific atoll near Hawaii. An old British sloop called *Sussex Rowan* had wrecked itself on a reef. The owner, Nick, along with his new wife Perri, were rescued and the boat, amazingly, salvaged and repaired.

After that, the internet is silent. But I take heart from the fact that Nick managed to break free from the pessimistic pages of Raban's book, and properly light out for the territories. Raban himself did so too, settling in Seattle and writing the marvellous, if terribly sad, *Passage to Juneau* about a voyage to Alaska on his newly-acquired ocean-going yacht.

Raban's boat in *Coasting* is an old wooden ketch called *Gosfield Maid*, a beautifully dumpy vessel designed and built in St Monans on the east coast of Scotland, patterned on a Scottish trawler and known as a Miller Fifer. Examples of this lovely class of boat come up for sale occasionally, at prices ranging from £25,000 upwards, and *Gosfield Maid* herself was advertised just a year or so ago. The pictures show a teak and mahogany interior, a nest for those who wish to rock themselves to sleep to the reassuring creak, crash and mutter of the sea. A *Swallows-and-Amazons*, Captain-Flint, Taffrail kind of haven for the fantasist who browses the dozens of yachting magazines available in any big city newsagent. I couldn't afford her in a thousand years, before even factoring in marina charges (remarkably cheap in Shetland) repairs, maintenance, and the banal fact that I had and have no idea how to sail a boat. Though I could learn. Here in Shetland, awash with 'pierhead skippers' and quite a few of the real thing, I could learn. There's Dave, who has his big yacht over at Skeld; Chris, who lives on a boat in Lerwick, though it must be admitted that he's never actually been out of the harbour in it. Or Nick, down in Southampton, my daughter-in-law's father, expert boatbuilder and international skipper. I could call him. Take a trip to Boulogne, or further, learn the ropes.

But I probably won't. Because here in the midst of the ocean, here in The Last Bookshop, the salt spray licks and whips at the windows, the gales rumble and howl around the eaves, and I can navigate by the stars as I pace the immovable stone decks of the ship I'm most comfortable in, at home in. Shetland itself.

*** *** ***

I wanted to mention the fishing industry, which in Shetland goes all the way from a one-man creel boat up to gigantic pelagic (oily fish such as mackerel and herring) supertrawlers, most of them concentrated on one island, the legendary place of modesty and money, Garansay.

Modest, these people, share-owners, many of them. Unboastful.

Despite the fact that the biggest, newest boats can cost £34 million. Sure, they can have nice houses, good cars. Clothes. The charity shop on Garansay is famous for the quality of its donated stock. But what are these skippers most proud of? Their boats. Boats with bridges which resemble those of science fiction spaceships. Boats that can make hundreds of thousands of pounds per trip.

And yet, at sea in a gale, loaded to the limit with fish, dealing with the danger and the threat, you wouldn't grudge them it. You can pretty much forgive them for the illegal landings, the amazing, true story of the fish factory in Lerwick which had a complete, secret conveyor belt and processing line for so-called 'blackfish'. The fines for skippers were astronomical, millions of pounds.

Meet them, they're affable, sociable, kind. There is, they argue, plenty of fish in the sea, plenty for everyone. Quotas? We know best. We're the ones out there, this is our lives, our futures. Yet they are ageing, now, and the stocks come and go, but mostly go. Big foreign companies sometimes move in and buy up the boats, and their valuable quota allowances for permissible catches. Their hobbies are often golf and... boating. There's nothing a fisherman likes more, when home from a long, dangerous trip, than going fishing. To *da eela*.

"Salt in the blood," one said to me, "salt in the blood." They're romantics, too. And they'd hate to admit, hate to read it here, but some of them are as wealthy as Croesus. You can tell by their fresh boiler suits and insulated wellies.

Rarity

By way of an aside, it's only fair to point out that one of the advantages of owning and operating The Last and Final Bookshop at The Edge of The World (Almost) is that I can write, sit around, watch daytime TV, make pieces of possibly saleable art, even do some gardening (within view of the front door), all while ostensibly shopkeeping.

Customers can come and go, and at this point, some time into the existence of this august establishment, I can point out that customers have come, and for that matter, gone. But while they come, browse, drink coffee and go, I can churn our poetry, prose, journalism, or letters to my heart's content and my fingers' fatigue on my little computer. The same computer I use to search for obscure model railway publications for my friend Chris, sell stuff on eBay, buy stuff from Biblio.com, or look for motorcycles to imagine myself zooming off to the South of France.

I mean, yes, I'm happy, I have found the meaning of life, but there is room in a bookshop for dreams. In fact, some would say that is what a bookshop is: a repository of dreams.

Right now, though, I want to talk about a nightmare. One that has just come to life. One that cost an unknown customer £15, and me potentially, £60.

It happens to every seller of rare books, I suppose. But this was sheer carelessness, and stupidity, and it took just three minutes following the departure of said customer (young, neat, wiped his feet, had pregnant girlfriend) clutching a fine/very fine (bookseller's coded ratings of condition: means just what it says) edition of Alastair Gray's *Old Negatives: Four Verse Sequences*, complete with dust jacket and spoof errata slip. Signed, limited edition of 500. I had priced it at £15, for various reasons: one, I got it for just a pound, dumped in a bargain bin in an Inverness bookshop, possibly as a joke by a visiting Alastair Gray, possibly because that's all it was worth; two, it's a very slight piece verging on self-indulgent rubbish, tarted up by Alastair's humorous book design and lovely litho cuts; three, I had – stupidly – not looked it up in RB Russell's *First Edition Prices*.

Which is what I did three minutes after selling it. To find it was priced at £75/35, depending on whether or not that limited edition, all signed, had its dust cover. Which this one, of course, did.

Now that customer, that young man, that bastard, may just have been an Alastair Gray fan, in which case he obtained a rather nice object to add to his collection, signed by the great man himself. Or he may have been a book dealer, or someone who knew a great deal more about rare books than me. Or had at least a working knowledge of prices.

I felt, for a brief moment, mildly sick. But then I thought – hell's teeth, it was never going to fetch £75 anyway. It was a bit rubbed. It's not as if it was the set of William Blake editions some acquaintances sold for £250,000, splitting the cash (with truly admirable honesty) with the hapless sucker who'd accepted £30 from them over the counter when he was trying to flog the things.

And after all, this is The Literary Finality at The Planet's Tipping Point, not Sotheby's.

Now, truth to tell, I'm a bit flushed and anxious, but recovering from my nausea. It's not even as if I'm £60 down on the deal. I'm £14 up. It's just that, if I'd only looked at the price guide… well. Maybe I'd still be sitting here with a lovely signed copy of *Old Negatives*, and not enough cash for a decent bottle of Tempranillo. What's more that neat young man has the book, but I have Last Books. And I know how much that's worth. Well, actually I don't. I couldn't put a price on it.

My wife knew Alastair Gray, author of the hugely influential but largely unread *Lanark* and the quite filthy *1982 Janine* (if you go for the original version, available, naturally, here at Ultimate

Volumes). She knew him quite well, and I used to see Alastair regularly when I was a west end of Glasgow barfly/whisky connoisseur/drunk. He was a customer of the Ubiquitous Chip (famously having painted a mural on the downstairs courtyard restaurant), in the upstairs bar of which I could found most evenings during them mid 1980s. I remember sitting in there once with my pal Seamus, when Alastair, whose appearance at the time could only be described as disreputable, appeared with a ferociously gorgeous, incredibly well-groomed young woman, possibly a publisher, agent or phD student from Finland, of which there were quite a few about. Or she may have been Estonian or from Wick.

Seamus, two Furstenbergs to the wind, eyed the shambling Alastair – now in laughing, intimate conversation with said blonde – balefully.

"What," Seamus bellowed, "has Benny Hill got that I haven't got?"

"A reputation as one of the greatest, possibly the greatest, Scottish writers of the 20th century, at least among creative writing tutors and failed authors, who are often the same thing," I replied. "And he's not a bad painter too."

Seamus contemplated this for a moment. "Aye well, maybe so," he said, eventually. "But my trousers are a lot cleaner than his. And my glasses aren't held together with Elastoplast."

Which was true enough. But didn't seem to be attracting the blonde woman to Seamus. Who did have exceptionally clean trousers. And wore contact lenses.

By this time you can probably tell that I am upset about making such a mess of valuing that copy of *Old Negatives*. But what can I say? I was careless, and sometimes you just fail miserably to get it right. Sometimes you just fail to recognise the value of what you have. Or had.

Take, for example, the folk-rock group Caedmon. The religious folk rock group Caedmon, a bunch of Edinburgh University students who, in the late 1970s, I knew quite well. The music they played was kind of ornate, gothic Fairport-Convention-meets-Horslips, full of Celtic references to Columcille and liable to break into jigs and reels at the least provocation. They had a very attractive girl singer and a strange guitarist who looked and played like a Celtic, ginger David Byrne. At the time, I was a keen (religious) folk musician too, and we would often play at the same gigs, at youth fellowship party evenings (pass the lemonade and the Bibles) University Christian Union socials, Women's Guild meetings, that sort of thing.

I was hideously jealous of Caedmon, as they'd made a record. On their own label, admittedly, but they'd gone to considerable lengths to make it an artistic and worthwhile artefact. It came in a complicated sleeve, with a free single, the A-side of which was a tune called *Only Jesus*. Despite being hideously jealous, I agreed to sell their record at gigs. It was, if I recall, £2.99, and one side of it was a conceptual piece about Columba which was worthy, complex and opaque. Kylie Minogue it wasn't. For my marketing efforts, they gave me a free sample.

Fast forward to the opening week of The Book (and Record) Shop at The Edge of The World, and here I am, checking through the records Francisco has given me to sell, using the *Record Collector Price Guide*. For some reason, my eye seizes on the entry for an Edinburgh folk rock band called Caedmon (not Caedmon's Call; that, weirdly, is an American Christian rock band and not to be entertained, or entertained by, or listened to). And there's that album. With free single *Only Jesus*, worth a cool £350.

Hell's teeth.

But all is not lost, I know I no longer possess that record, as it was in the collection of LPs I owned together with my first wife. I email David, one of the two now-grown sons we had, and ask him to check if the LP is among the records he inherited from his late mother. Two days later, he gets back to me: it is there. But the free single has vanished, inevitably. And, he adds, "there appears to be some handwriting on the sleeve... can't make out what it says, but it looks suspiciously like yours..." The worth of the album has plummeted with every word. Even more so than books, records need to be mint if they're to fetch their 'book' values.

Much later, I get the chance to see what it was I wrote on the cover of that Caedmon album. I decipher the words 'Remember Guild 12-string Biggars payment'. Hire purchase on a guitar, the risk of bankruptcy. Happy days. Because of my vandalism, it might be worth £20.

Catalogue valuations are pretty vague commodities anyway. I've just sold one of Francisco's albums on eBay – Steeleye Span's first LP, *Hark! The Village Wait*, on the original RCA label, book value £35. It went for £6. To a man in Finland called Nikka, who is probably not related to that woman Alastair Gray was having a drink with all those years ago.

Alastair Gray, eh? *Old Negatives* worth £75. Who'd have believed THAT?

Stupid. Stupid, stupid, stupid, stupid, STUPID!

Still, I'm happy. I've found the meaning of life. I don't really care if I don't sell any books, as long as I can sit here among them. Here in The Ultimate Print Repository, Depository, Suppository. Joy consumes. I am content.

Two weeks later, a message arrives from David. He's sold that Caedmon album, complete with my casual inscription, on eBay. For £270.

Stove

The Dutch word *gezillig* is one of my favourites in any language (pronounced *he-SILL-ick* or, I was taught in Seeland, very Scottishly as *chhh-SILL-icchhh*). Its meaning, however, is as slippery as a twitching mackerel in the bottom of a fourareen. According to Wikipedia, it represents "a perfect example of untranslatability... (it) does not have an English equivalent. Literally, it means cosy, quaint, or nice, but can also connote time spent with loved ones, seeing a friend after a long absence, or general togetherness."

People can be *gezillig*, or to be precise, *gezillige*. A restaurant can be *gezillig* or *ongezillig*, depending on whether or not it is, say, The Peerie Shop Café or the (unbuilt) Lerwick branch of Burger King. On the other hand, any branch of Burger King (or McDonalds, or KFC) can be *gezillig* if you're in a group of *gezillige* pals.

When I visited the Netherlands years ago I was conscious of the cosiness and, well, compact and bijou nature of the houses in which I stayed. It was explained to me that was a *gezillig* thing. I fell in love with many aspects of Dutch life, notably vla, the truly wondrous thin custard which, when I was there, you had delivered to your door in bottles with milk and a lovely drinking yoghurt. Gathered around the kitchen table, mixing the two and drinking strong black coffee... well, that was almost the definition of *gezillig*-ness.

Shetland of course has very strong links with Holland – Lerwick was founded in the 17th century by the Dutch herring fishermen who used to anchor each season in Bressay Sound. We do not, alas, have our own version of vla, though the traditional Shetland drink blaand (fermented milk) sounds similar and is in some ways similar to that thin drinking yoghurt.

But if Shetland has Dutch connections, it has stronger ones with Scandinavia, and the fashionable Danish concept of *hygge* is, if not identical with, closely related to *gezillig*. *Hygge* is defined as 'the art of intimacy – a feeling or mood that comes from taking genuine pleasure in making ordinary, everyday things more meaningful, beautiful or special.' I always think of it as more about interior design and, that horrid word, lifestyle, than genuine, enforced cosiness due to the necessities of a winter way of life. The Shetland dialect phrase 'in aboot da night' conjures up for me the loveliest aspects of a winter in the northernmost Scottish isles, particularly when it becomes an invitation (or a demand): "Cam ye aa in aboot da night." It's untranslatable, but essentially means: "Come, on, everybody, come into the house, sit down next to the Rayburn and have a glass of this dark rum, a cup of tea, large amounts of soup, mutton, bread, butter and homemade cakes of every variety, and listen to some stories, tell some stories, gossip, sing, play tunes on the fiddle and guitar. Or share my curry and watch this new Netflix series. More rum? Perhaps a Red Tin or an obscure and tasty local IPA?" I told you it was untranslatable.

The key to this essential notion of hospitality is, for me, the Rayburn. Or shall we just say 'stove'? I think we shall. There are Mørsos, Stanleys, Charnwoods and even in the poshest of households, Agas (Aga actually own Rayburn these days, and have tried to convert that workpersonlike brand into an upmarket, *hygge*-laden icon of aspiration). It should be peat fired, as the pungent aroma, the reek of burning bog is part of the winter isles experience.

It should be so hot it glows red, and controllable to the extent that it does not set the chimney on fire. In the past, it would have been the absolute epicentre of family life, providing food, heat, hot water and refuge from the darkness and cold (often moving very quickly) outside. It would never go out, except on the cusp of the aald new year, when it would be symbolically extinguished before being relit for the coming 12 months.

Now, in our house, the stove is a symbol of welcome, warmth and winter. It is pure *gezillig*, except when it's unlit, cold and badly needing emptied of ash, when it is very definitely *ongezillig*. And devoid of *hygge*. So excuse me, but I must go and sort out the Rayburn, sorry stove. It's lunchtime, it's getting dark and there are folk coming round. I have custard to cook.

*** *** ***

Burning peat is one of the great pleasures and miseries of life in Shetland. And not just in winter. Spring too requires the Rayburn (I don't know of anyone in Shetland who has an Aga; that would be too, too posh even though it's one and the same company these days) to be fired up, sending (if it gets hot enough, and it doesn't always) warm water gurgling along the pipes to radiators and taking a little of the pressure off our super-expensive oil boiler.

And yes, I know none of this is eco-friendly, that both oil and peat are carbon fuels at different stages of development, but I take comfort from the fact that our peat is cut, dried, raised, turned, stacked, bagged and then transported home from just a mile or so away. By hand. By us, or mostly. You've heard of slow food? This is slow fuel.

Shetland, of course, is amply supplied with peat bogs, an adequate sufficiency for there not be too much pressure on the ecological treasures held there and having to be carefully guarded elsewhere. Nobody is harvesting the stuff industrially, as in Ireland, and many crofters regard 'the machine' (usually an attachment for a tractor that produces long cylinders of extruded peat) with suspicion. Peat cutting is a tradition as old as the human community in the isles, and one surrounded with rules, regulations and traditions. You have to ca' canny with your tushker, or tuskir (almost the same word in Gaelic), the tool used to cut each slab of brown, black or – much treasured – blue compacted and aged vegetable matter, one step or a few million years or so from turning into coal.

The peat banks in any country area of Shetland are under

crofting tenure, usually on common grazings administered by the local grazings committee. The days of the 'peat constable' whose job it was to enforce digging and cutting rules may have gone, but heaven help you if you trespass on someone else's banks. When we first arrived in our little community we applied for permission to cut peats and were told to use the old, and uncut for many years, Church of Scotland Manse banks. I began fleeing or flaying them in preparation (removing the top layer of turf or heather; you keep these to restore the cut bank when you're finished), and when I returned next day I found that stern warning signs had been erected, hand-painted in blood red, by an elderly and – when I met him – absolutely raging gentleman who had not been party to the grazings committee decision. The minister was consulted, doubtless prayers were said, and we were eventually given permission to proceed.

As it turned out, we gave up on peat for a few years and when we started looking at solid fuel again, having installed a second-hand Rayburn with a back boiler, we were given banks much nearer the road and thus more convenient for transporting them home. Which didn't stop me nearly losing a very expensive Nissan Patrol four wheel drive when trying to tow away a trailer full of fuel. Moral: don't drive on the bright green bits!

And of course, the house we're trying to heat is in fact the old Church of Scotland Manse, the minister having long departed and indeed, services at the local kirk having alas been reduced to the barest minimum. The kirk banks, too – as I say, a wee bit awkward to get to – have become overgrown and almost unrecognisable.

But who knows? They may once again become a source of warmth and comfort for someone, as more and more Shetlanders are turning away from oil and electricity (there is only bottled gas) towards a fuel that is only expensive in time and sweat. And, on occasion, a bit too damp to catch fire readily.

*** *** ***

I am bored with windfarms. Tidal energy? Wave power? The Orcadians have stolen a march, or a tidal race, on Shetland even though our tides and waves are of course far, far better and racier than those belonging to the inorganic beef farmers of the southern isles.

Who needs salt water? For the last few weeks I have been consumed with thoughts of a far more immediate, less engineering-heavy source of energy. I speak, of course, of peat.

As I write, I have just returned from the first of what will probably be nine visits to the hill, there to load the already raised and mostly dry peat onto the trailer of my Goldoni two-wheeled tractor (Mediterranean Merry Tiller, known as Lascivia and an evil, vicious machine from hell. Or to be precise, Italy). Our peat banks are a tortuous and boggy 100 metres or so from the nearest passing place, and easier access has been denied us by the council's Ditch Department, back in the days (two years ago) when it was intent on digging enormous trenches beside every Shetland road and eradicating all forms of wild flower infestation. Fortunately, the council no longer has a ditch department. It has been ditched, so that the money saved can be ploughed into the maintenance of consultative iPad trials and the medical insertion of communications devices into the skulls of councillors. Or brains.

Anyway, what I have to do is put the tiller/trailer on a road trailer, tow it to the peat bank, unload it, trundle my way to the raised peats, fill it, wrestle my way back to the passing place, transfer the peats, and repeat six times in all until the big trailer is full. That's about two and a half hours of work. Back to the house and, peat by peat, stack the brown horrors.

Now, I know that something is missing from this scenario. And that something is bags. Plastic fertiliser or sheep or salmon feed bags, the classic method of transferring peats home. I hate them with a great hatred. I hate the way they grow brittle and break, but only once you've filled and are lifting them. I hate the way they fill with water, re-soggifying the dried peats. I hate the fact that they add several more processes to the already ludicrously human-heavy business of using peat as a domestic fuel (pleading with somebody for bags, fetching them, taking them to the hill, unfolding and filling them, lifting the full bags onto a barrow, barrowing them to the road, stacking the bags, lifting them onto a trailer, lifting them off a trailer, emptying them). Admittedly we have a neighbour who has offered to quad-bike-and-trailer our peats to the road but that still involves hand-bagging. As opposed to handbagging which is totally inefficient. The leather just won't take the strain.

Two years ago, I crazily bought several hundred net sacks designed to carry logs. These proved even more susceptible to light than plastic feed bags. They had the tensile strength of toilet roll after a few days on the hill. I wept peaty tears of rage as they failed time and time again. Scraps of these horrendous items still blow up and down Hjalda Voe, and may even have been swallowed by salmon and incorrectly identified as parasitic orange worm infestations.

Anyway. Six wee Goldoni trailerfuls of peat make one big road-trailerful. I estimate nine more Ifor-Williamsfuls to get the rest of the peat home. I am treating it as a penance. I am contemplating ponies and kishies. And of course, while engaged in this work, I have been thinking. And the future of Shetland is of course, not wind, not wave, not tidal, not the ridiculous notion of imported wood. It is peat.

Back in the 1970s, just pre-oil, it was suggested that Yell, 55 square miles of which is covered in peat to a depth of at least five feet in old money, could become the site for a peat-fired power station. This was in the end rejected in the face of black gold's arrival. Now, peat power stations are nothing new, though it is generally argued these days that burning peat is a heinous environmental sin, second only to eating dolphin-poodle stew, as is common in Faroe, where the ceremony of the mass poodle slaughter is a much loved annual event. And dolphin farming is common.

But Estonia has a modern peat-and-biomass fired power station, so does Finland, and there is a sneaky way in Scandinavia of planting your used peat bogs with Reed Canary Grass which can be harvested, turned into briquettes and used as fuel, or processed to produce the psychedelic drug dimethyltryptamine, which is like LSD and makes you feel like you're inhabiting an alien planet. Some would say that's entirely unnecessary in Yell, but who am I to comment?

You must admit, this is a much more interesting prospect than awful oil, tedious tidal or woeful, bird-chopping windfarms. Hallucinogenic electricity, made from peat and plants! The aroma of peat reek, wafting across Yell Sound! And just think of the spin-off industries, like tushkar manufacture, kishie-making and pony breeding.

Because obviously Goldoni two-wheeled tractors wouldn't be appropriate. Besides. They're rubbish, and I hate them. Want to buy one?

Tabnabs

It is a wonder and a glory, one of the greatest aspects of life in Shetland, and it involves, as you may have guessed, food. I am talking about the 'hall tea', which can sometimes merge effortlessly into the 'school tea' or just 'eight o'clocks' which may happen at 8.00pm, or earlier, or later. But what we are really talking about is home baking.

In summer, the 'Sunday hall tea' is a weekly event in one or other corner of the isles, with local women and men baking and staffing a Sabbath afternoon extravaganza at one of the (oil-funded and rather luxurious) Shetland community halls, from Unst in the north to Sumburgh in the south. You pay a set amount, usually, and can then drink as much tea or coffee as you like, filling your plate beyond the brim with sandwiches, quiche, pie, scones, bannocks and 'fancies', which can mean anything from cupcakes to gateaux, chocolate crispy crunches to brownies. Surpluses are sold as takeaways. It is a fantastic opportunity not to cook, and to guess who baked what if you're a member of the local community concerned.

This past week has seen a hall tea and a school sale in Quidawick, both fuelled by baking of the highest possible standard. Two legends of bannock making, Roger Montrose and Nina Tracey, had examples of their work at the 'Bake it for the Beatson' (the centre for cancer treatment in Glasgow, one many Shetlanders and soothmoothers have cause to be grateful to) event on Sunday, an opportunity for bannock connoisseurs such as myself. The Shetland bannock is a kind of buttermilk-fuelled scone which can be griddled or oven-cooked, or sometimes both. There are as many recipes and twists to the basic technique as there are puffins on the cliffs, but a good starting point is Margaret Stout in the book *Cookery for Northern Wives*, for Beremeal (a particular kind of flour made from the extremely hardy for of barley known as bere) bannocks:

Ingredients:

400g beremeal
200g plain wheat flour
(Or 600g of the special 'Voe Bannock Flour', only available in Shetland, which is self-raising, but which has nothing do with beremeal)

1 pinch salt
1 teaspoon of baking powder (or not; this is a matter of debate)
Buttermilk (readily available fresh from Shetland Dairies)

Method:

Mix dry ingredients
Add enough buttermilk to make a soft dough
Knead gently and divide into lumps
Flatten and divide into scone-like smaller lumps (not too thick unless you like them that way)
Heat a griddle or thick pan, preferably not greasing with a little oil. But if you insist.
Cook the small lumps on one side for 3-5 minutes. I like them burnt.
Turn them over and cook the other side.
The bannock rises as it cooks. If it sounds hollow when tapped, it's ready. Wrap in a cloth to keep warm and soft. Serve with butter.

Eat immediately. Toastable within one day. After that, they're pigfood.

(This probably won't work; and while beremeal is traditional, some say it's horrible.)

There was, perhaps inevitably, an overabundance of excellent baking on Sunday, and as Susan was one of the organisers, we purchased a lot to take home for freezing. Thursday was school sale day, again with lots of terrific baking, as well as the availability of commercially-produced Vidlin Pies. The eating has been good this week. But as one friend and neighbour said as we packed everything away on Thursday, "I'm a' fancied oot!"

It passes, though, that sensation. And then you may feel, between and betwixt meals, peckish. Time, to use old naval parlance, for *tabnabs*. Cakes, biscuits, sweetmeats, savoury pies of a small and sustaining variety. And if you can't be bothered making them yourself, why not head to the village of Voe (source of the aforementioned bannock flour) for a box of their best. The bakery was founded, after all, during World War One, solely to supply the Royal Navy's Grand Cruiser Squadron with tabnabs, bread and other forms of floury delight. And it's still going strong.

*** *** ***

Food memory. It's a funny thing, our ability to recall the shape, texture and taste of particular foods. Childhood taste experiences not only resonate down the years, but influence our adult food choices. We seek out the morsels which recreate past, innocent pleasures.

And sometimes, food memory deceives. Of late I've been eating Jacob's Club Orange biscuits reasonably often, for one simple reason: my wife hates them, and so does my daughter, who was home for the summer. Therefore I could guarantee a secure supply of sweetmeats was lurking in the fridge when I came in from my daily grind of mild dogwalking, in need of a snacky sugar rush.

Memory played its part, of course. Club biscuits were as near a chocolate bar, a proper sweet, as you could get when I was a child in the 1960s, and cheaper than a Mars or a Crunchie.

71

But I've gradually become aware that the Club biscuit is different these days. I always recall it as squat, brick-like, very chocolatey, very crunchy. It still has a hint of that, but it has definitely slimmed down. It's thinner, there's less chocolate. I didn't realise the reasons for that, or that the Club is mired in fear, loathing, hatred, anti-French sentiment, anti- (and pro-) Irish sentiment.

It all starts in Ireland, where, just prior to World War One, WR Jacobs started producing the 'Club Milk' biscuit from a tiny bakery in Waterford. They quickly moved to Dublin and grew. It was a classic format: two biscuits sandwiching cocoa cream, surrounded by thick layer of milk chocolate, wrapped in foil and then a slip wrap of paper. Within a year it was being made and marketed in the UK, from the company's Liverpool factory. By the 1920s, the UK and Irish branches were operating separately.

The range expanded (orange, fruit, mint, plain) and became hugely popular in the UK, until in 1970 the Irish and British divisions of Jacobs were separated. If you're old enough you may still remember the 'playing card' packaging used for the original biscuit, which provided the name 'Club' in the first place.

"If you want a lot of chocolate on your biscuit, join our club." The jingle was everywhere and there WAS a lot of chocolate on a Club. You could nibble it off leaving the biscuit layers shorn and naked. Oh, and despite many west of Scotland jokes, Orange Clubs had and have no sectarian connotations.

Disaster struck in the mid-1990s when French firm Danone bought both the Irish and British branches of Jacobs. They changed everything: the packaging (no foil, no paper, just cellophane) and the recipe. One biscuit, less cocoa cream, a different, thinner layer of 'chocolate-based coating'. There was outrage. Sacre Bleu!

In 2004 things got complicated. Danone sold the UK arm of Jacobs to United Biscuits who reinstated the packaging but left the skinflint French single-biscuit recipe intact. The Irish arm was sold to the Fruitfield Group, and Jacob Fruitfield Foods was formed, who are now marketing the original Jacob's Milk Club, made exactly according to its full-thickness, double-biscuit, real chocolate recipe. There are stories of legal action in Ireland to stop cheaper (and inferior) biscuits being imported. And Jacobs in the UK are apparently in frequent legal 'communication' with Jacob Fruitfield over the use of the name on a number of other lines (like Cream Crackers, for instance; you can see how confusion could arise). As for availability of the 'Original Milk Club' in the UK, that would be a question of not The Last Bookshop, but Amazon, where you can buy them. £35 for a minimum order of 60 biscuits. Maybe I should get them in stock.

In 2008, the massive old Jacob's factory in Tallaght, Ireland, closed, although biscuits are still being made elsewhere. As for Shetland, I have both Mint and my wife-alienating Orange Club, and obviously I quite like them. The thing is, before researching this piece, I had no yearning for the old, higher, double-sandwich, real chocolate pre-Danone version. My taste memory had been traduced.

Now I want them back. Now I remember.

Light

The light comes in, days lengthen, midnight skies turn dark blue, then indigo, then pale pink or creamy grey. It's May, and after the last rattle of hail, the final flutter of snow, comes a sudden blast of warmth.

At last the rhubarb is long enough to be worth harvesting, and at this time of year it's sweet and tender. Puddings are sorted now until September, beyond if there's a surplus, and there nearly always is, and there's room in the freezer. Crumbles, pies, sorbets, stewed breakfast toppings, fools, yoghurts; amazing concoctions involving rhubarb cooked with mutton and mackerel, though not at the same time. Once considered so precious by the Chinese, people died to stop it being smuggled to the west. Now endemic in Shetland, unstoppable, unkillable, glorious. Appearing to grow inches from day to day, rhubarb is the sour, sharp sweetness of summer, even for gardeners lacking green fingers.

Green toes. And ankles. That's an issue for those of us with grass to cut. From now until October it's every week, and the struggle to start reluctant mowers leads to pounding hearts, barked knuckles and much swearing. Finally, the engines smoke into life, and the endless tramping around lawns begins, the careful cutting into stripes of greensward, the dumping of cuttings on tattie beds to induce warmth and quicker growth. Along with the kelp, gathered from beaches after storms, washed and dried.

The days grow hotter, longer still, and you can find yourself up to two grass-cuts a week, mulch ingrained into sandled feet, or up shins if you've given in, unwisely to the temptation of shorts.

How hot can Shetland get? How sunny. May can be amazing. In

1992, suncream supplies ran out as the weeks went on and the skies remained unbelievably blue. And unusually, Shetland was aligned with mainland Scotland, where it was the warmest May since 1833. The heatwave began on the 13th, when very warm southerly winds from North Africa embraced the entire country. Under the clear sunny skies, temperatures soared into the high 20s and Scotland had its warmest day for that year on the 14th, with Glasgow recording 26.8C, Aviemore 25.9C and Edinburgh an amazing 28.9C.

Shetland? Well, Shetland for once avoided the curse of the fog, the seamist, the haar. It just felt cooler because of the breeze. That's the issue if you're wandering about on a fine day that feels cool. You're still getting burnt. This was spelt out to me the first time I went peat-cutting, and returned so stiff and scarred with sunburn I couldn't sleep for two calamine lotion-drenched nights in succession.

In 2009, things got a little out of hand. It was the warmest June ever, or at least since records began. More than 240 hours of sunshine. In 1959, there had been a mere 236. Again, there was an absence of that frequent sense of local grievance at the rest of Scotland for being sunny when Shetland was flightless and sightless. No fog. A maximum temperature of 21.7 C, and even a night when things never cooled beyond 14 degrees. It was another occasion when emergency supplies of sunscreen had to be ordered in as shops sold out. The Gilbert Bain Hospital had to deal with three cases of severe sunburn at the accident and emergency department. Cool off in the sea? Why not? For a minute or two. Survival time in Shetland coastal waters, even in these conditions, can be as short at 30 minutes' total immersion. Be careful.

This year? Who knows? On 9th May, ill-advised amounts of skin were exposed by workers and tourists alike as a combination of blue skies, heat and stillness brought a near-tropical atmosphere and a very swift dearth of barbecue supplies. In Ramnavine, the demand for local man Roger Montrose's upcycled truck-wheel barbecues and firepits made from old washing machine drums reached fever pitch. Charcoal ran out. Sausages were changing hands at inflated prices, or might have been had any been available.

Meanwhile, the cutting and raising of peats continues. Activity is not as fervid as it has been in recent years, what with the oil price being so low, but the competition for peat banks near the road, and hence easier to exploit, remains fierce. Do not fall out with the grazings committee which allocates the banks, or the forces of law may be invoked! Call the peat constable! Or better, don't. Sort it out among yourselves.

As the peats dry and are then carted home, thoughts turn towards the coming winter; the slow, then faster and faster dimming of the days.

Because even in the midst of light, we are in darkness. We know it in our hearts. Winter is coming.

***   ***   ***

Mist. Haar. *Stumba*, in Shetland dialect. A *steekit stumba* is a mist so thick you can hardly see through it. And I write in the season for it, as darkness begins to fall and the cooling atmosphere condenses droplets of water into opaque greyness.

I love the misty mornings, the gathering billows of fog of an evening, the way light in its varied forms, from breaking dawn through blazing sun to the pink and orange of sunset, all produce a range of complex effects that leave you stunned by their loveliness.

Of course mist can and does have its drawbacks. Those of a superstitious or easily frightened nature will find it difficult to erase memories of John Carpenter's film *The Fog*, and the zombie pirates massing to take a terrible revenge on the village that brought about their doom. But this happens all the time in Shetland and we've grown used to it. Besides, our vikings sorted out those pesky pirates a while ago.

And then there are the flight delays. Yes, I know. Horribly inconvenient, but if it provides you with an extra day or, ah, three in these gorgeous northern isles, can you really complain?

Tonight we drove up to Karaness, hoping to catch, as we have in the past, the dappling of the entire sky in flaming orange that happens when the sun dips below the horizon and catches the forming fog above. The sun shimmered, perfectly round and blood red, then vanished into a thick bank of haar. We went for a walk anyway, from the lighthouse west, in the nightfall breeze. And then, coming back in the car, saw the full moon catching the *stumba*-filtered pinkness of the sunset.

And so back home, the lyrics to Nick Drake's wondrous song running through our heads:

Saw it written and I saw it say
Pink Moon is on its way
And none of you stand so tall
Pink Moon gonna get you all.

Copyright Nick Drake, 1974. Island Music Publishing.

Power

Here at The Last Bookshop, power cuts can happen at any time of year. They're caused, most often in our neck of the bog, by high winds driving anything remotely conductive (salt water, fresh water, snow, hail, ice, bits of corrugated iron, caravans) against the overhead lines, shorting them out.

We are prepared. Usually. There's a petrol generator in the shed, and sometimes there's petrol for it too. We keep candles and electric torches in various drawers; occasionally we have batteries for the torches and can remember where the candles are. Our 'Hydro Men' (now wearing SSE uniforms, and they needn't be males) are blessedly efficient and seemingly impervious to bad weather. It's rare for the power not come back on within a few hours.

In my 1960s Glasgow childhood, where there were few flying caravans, electricity seemed flickeringly erratic. "The fusebox!" my mum would shout, and as matches were struck, one by one, the search would be on for wire to replace the tiny sliver that had just melted, usually because my dad's power drill, in near-constant use and of which he was inordinately proud, had overheated again in the course of incessant woodworking.

To be honest, I'm a bit hazy on fusewire replacement techniques, though I do remember visiting one flat in the 1970s where the inhabitants announced proudly that the fuses had been replaced with silver paper and nails. Engineering students, eh? These people are probably running the country nowadays.

My student flat, in a curious twist, was the top floor of my old childhood home. My dad was a dentist in Pollokshaws, Glasgow, with the surgery in a front room of the house we lived in. By 1962 a third child had arrived, the surgery was growing busier, and most of the old 'shaws tenements were being razed to the ground. The Morton family moved to Troon, and dentistry took over the entire ground floor of the house, leaving a two-room flat above. It was there I lived from 1973 while I was at Glasgow University.

I don't remember any power cuts, but I do distinctly recall watching what must have been one of the very last 'leerie men' doing his rounds of an evening, carrying a long brass rod with which to light the stair gas mantles in the tenements opposite. In just the same way as a very young Robert Louis Stevenson had watched *The Lamplighter* in the previous century:

My tea is nearly ready and the sun has left the sky.
It's time to take the window to see Leerie going by;
For every night at teatime and before you take your seat,
With lantern and with ladder he comes posting up the
street...

Those Mannering Road gas lamps must have been some of the last in the city. Though the Leerie Man later became electrified, so to speak, travelling with a special spanner to switch on the stair power. Some of the old tenement close electricity boxes can still be seen on the pavements of Glasgow, where power cuts are now rare, and the old fuse box has given way to a row of circuit breakers. No longer do young flat-renters use safety pins or nails instead of fusewire. Not even the engineering students.

There are still leerie men alive and working, far south of here in the City of London, where 1500 gas lamps still illuminate the streets every night. Some of these cast iron and glass, thoroughly Narnian wonders are up to 200 years old, and a necklace of them stretches from Bromley-by-Bow in the East End to Richmond Bridge in the west. The unique mellow glow of the gas mantles brings history to life – or rather, the five full-time leerie men, the last in the UK, do.

I still have a gas lamp, here in the bookshop. Just a wee

Camping Gaz affair, but it hisses and produces that amazing purity of light you just don't get from pink or yellow electric bulbs. Hurricane or pressure lanterns, running on paraffin, are still popular among older crofters – always Tilley lanterns in Shetland, though there are many other makes like Aladdin – and there's now a bit of a collector's market for them. It would be a kind of *hygge* thing, I suppose, if they weren't so dangerous. They can spill, leak, explode, set houses and people on fire. And they're smelly. But some people can't see past them for pure, aromatic, 'natural' lighting nostalgia. Refurbished ones are available online, 'fully tested', for £55.

And this is where I whisper that for reading in power cuts, there really is nothing like a backlit Kindle Paperwhite e-book reader.

I can't believe I just said that.

Flight

You walk out onto the tarmac at Sumburgh Airport in Shetland, and it can be like the final scene in Casablanca. Only colder, obviously. A lot colder. And nobody wears a homburg hat, like Humphrey Bogart, as it would disappear in an instant, to be eaten by seabirds.

And not that it's a Lockheed Electra 12-A, Ingrid Bergman's transportation, you'll be boarding as you head for points south – Aberdeen, Orkney, Inverness, Glasgow or Edinburgh. Loganair, who do the actual flying in FlyBe livery, use Saab 340 aircraft. The model number '340' has always slightly worried me, as one of the oddest cars I ever owned was a Volvo 340, the belt-drive model formerly made by Dutch manufacturer DAF, and considered something of a joke. Still, the Saabs seem to work, and they are similar to the 'we'll always have Paris' aeroplane in that they have two propellers. I do like a propeller. There's something about watching it turning around that provides reassurance. Until, of course, it stops.

I was brought up with visits to airports – mainly Renfrew and Prestwick – as major childhood treats. Not that there was ever any possibility of actually going 'up' in an aeroplane. That was unthinkable, and reserved for the very rich, the very famous and people who, like my dad, had been in the RAF. True, he had been a dentist in the RAF, but had actually sat beside the pilot when he cadged lifts from Feltwell in Norfolk back home to Glasgow. And then there was my never-known grandfather, a sergeant pilot in the early days of the RAF, trained and just about to head for France when the armistice came.

So we would go to Renfrew or Prestwick and just look. I don't even remember seeing many take-offs or landings, though that was always phenomenally exciting. Especially (in the early 1960s) when they extended one of the Prestwick runways and there was a level crossing system installed on the Monkton to Prestwick road. Cars had to wait until the aeroplane had passed. We bairns were beside ourselves with excitement, and curiously I still have vivid dreams about those rare events.

Probably fuelled by the fact that, when driving to Sumburgh Airport, you have to stop at a rather more modern set of traffic lights and barrier, as the airport access road crosses the main runway. I believe Shetland is the last place in the UK this happens – there used to be a back road crossing Wick Airport in Caithness and it is still the case I think that the main road into Gibraltar from Spain has to be closed every time there's a take-off or landing.

But air travel has become so much a part of our daily lives, and security such an issue, that simply watching aeroplanes is regarded with extreme and understandable suspicion. Observation decks – remember them? – are shut throughout the world. Teenage boys with shortwave radios are never seen lurking at perimeter fences, or if they are they're soon arrested by armed police, and searched for rocket propelled grenades or, at the very least, the dreaded laser pen.

It seems a shame that the mystery, joy and glamour of just watching wondrous technology in action has vanished. Still, when I climb onto a Saab 340 for the trip to Glasgow, I do feel a tremor of excitement.

Or maybe it's just fear…

Wildlife

When I first arrived in Shetland, some 38 years ago, I was barely interested in wildlife and birds not at all. I knew the difference between a starling and a robin, just about. I could tell a killer whale from a dolphin, because one was called Namu (from the 1966 movie, not the later and inferior Orca films) and the other Flipper, from the Australian TV series. As a child, I was obsessed with both Flipper and what I thought of as his near-cousin Skippy the Bush Kangaroo, though it turned out, sadly, they were unrelated.

There were and are no kangaroos in Shetland (though there are, oddly enough, feral wallabies in Scotland, on an island in Loch Lomond). Dolphins, porpoises, killer whales and other sea mammals abound in the seas around our coastline, and it can get to the point where you kind of take sightings for granted. I remember once having the eminent BBC naturalist Arnolfini Duchesse in my car, during one of his first visits to Shetland, and he became so excited at a report that a pod of orcas had been seen off Karaness that we ended up rushing around Ramnavine in a frenzy of binocular-brandishing and texting. We didn't see them. I, frankly wasn't too bothered. I have a slight issue with killer whales. It's the prefix 'killer'. I do a lot of sea kayaking in the summer and the thought of being surrounded, all of a sudden, by a top-of-the-food-chain group of ultra-predators whilst paddling around the entrance to Stamar Voe is a mite disturbing. The father of a friend, out on 'da eela' (inshore fishing) in a small, open Shetland Model boat once found himself amid an orca pod and it's fair to say that it left him somewhat concerned. Yes, I know they're not known to attack human beings, but what are you supposed to do if one takes a nibble at your neoprene wetsuit? Shout "leave me alone, I'm not a seal, honestly"? Perhaps that would work. They are supposed to be highly intelligent creatures. Maybe they speak English. With a Shetland accent.

My early education in The Ways of Shetland began with an introduction to the word 'twitcher', which I had never even heard previously. This was because a group of said uber-birdie-folk gathered with their monoculars, cameras and notebooks outside our garden in Voe which was, at the time, one of the few patches of forest in Shetland. To be honest, it still is. There had been a report. Of A Bird. Who knows what rare straggler it was? This was in the pre-internet days, when information on rare feathered sightings was relayed through groups in staged telephone calls. But then, as now, wealthy enthusiasts would charter aircraft to add something particularly tasty (not that they would ever eat it) to their life list.

Gradually, I gained enough knowledge to tell the difference between a puffin and a 'Norwegian Blue' parrot ('beautiful plumage'). The cat dragging a whimbrel onto the doorstep as a gift was enough to necessitate a swift burial (of the bird) in order to prevent said feline's assassination by our more ornithomaniac friends. But there were moments when seeing a wild creature for the first time brought an overwhelming thrill, a sense of wonder.

The slinky slither of an otter as it slipped through the garden towards the sea took my breath away. Suddenly I was thinking back to the film, *Ring of Bright Water*, and that itself provoked a reading of Gavin Maxwell's amazing books, set in Arnisdale on the Scottish west coast. They are beautiful animals, but no-one who has read the hideous story of how the late TV naturalist Terry Nutkins, at 15 an assistant to Maxwell, had two fingers bitten off by the pet Maxwell otter Edal, would ever touch one. It's a tale which haunts my nightmares, as you can probably guess. Recently, I met an elderly Shetlander who used to hunt them for their skins.

"We would fill our wellington boots with ash, so they couldn't bite through into our legs," he told me. Something with jaws capable of crunching a crab shell like fudge is to be treated with great respect, even if it does look like a sleekit meerkat.

It's easy to idealise, anthropomorphise Shetland's wildlife. Most of them are anything but cuddly, though. And sometimes, they can frighten, and leave you with a sense of awe.

That was my experience with certainly the biggest animal I have ever encountered. A number of years ago in Burra, a blue whale became disorientated, trapped, then stranded. A blue whale is not just big. It's the largest creature ever to have existed on earth, anything up to 30 metres long and 200 tonnes in weight – though no-one has ever actually weighed one, at least not in a single piece. Bigger than the biggest known dinosaur. Hunted almost to extinction, and now protected but still utterly mysterious.

I was alone on the beach, watching this vast mammal surface, and I felt suddenly diminished, as if I were shrinking, tiny and insignificant. Weirdly, I felt the same way just last week, when there was a shrieking in our garden, then silence. Looking out from the porch, I could see a female sparrowhawk regarding me balefully as she tore lumps out of the blackbird she had just killed. Predator. Raptor. Killer. Another piece of the Un-Human, completely indifferent to my existence, and utterly superior.

I still know very little about birds, fish and wandering wild animals. I have my favourites, though. Rupert the Redshank will be back soon, and the whooper swans are always a treat to watch. I love the Shetland names like dunter (eider), maali (fulmar), leerie (manx shearwater) and scarf (shag). Call me an infant, but even saying the word 'shag' makes me laugh. Grey herons (haigrie), the gangly Steerpikes of the avian world, are somehow a delight, and spring has not arrived properly until the tirricks (arctic terns) return from their annual sojourn in the Antarctic.

One event, though, in 1993 made me realise how much I felt for Shetland and its non-human inhabitants. That was the wreck of the tanker *Braer* at Garths Ness in the South Mainland.

I had recently left Shetland to live and work in the Highlands as a national news journalist. My newspaper chartered a private plane and I flew into Sumburgh in a force 11 gale to cover the story. I watched as the Braer, helpless and abandoned, came ashore, its fuel tanks already ruptured and the air a filthy, moving mass of hydrocarbons. Next morning it was calm, and the south mainland coastline was thick, toxic, jellied and black. I stopped the car at the Sand of Hayes, and realised that the slow, treacly waves were laden with dead fish and birds, hundreds, thousands of them. Old Douglas DC3 aircraft swooped mere feet from the surface, dropping detergent to no obvious effect. Distraught friends wept at the sight. For once I could identify some of the dead and dying birds, and that made things worse.

An enormous effort saved a few oil-damaged birds, otters and seals. A scouring hurricane cleared away the worst of the pollution. Now, you wouldn't know the *Braer* had ever happened. But anyone who was there knows the terrible cost.

And now, every time I see a bird, an otter, a whale, a dolphin or a seal, I'm grateful it hasn't happened again, and that I'm here to see Shetland and its native wildlife for the most part clean, pure and healthy. I count the cost. And I name the species. Whaap, bonxie, peerie maa. I'm still learning.

Sinking

It's 2007, and I'm shouting at the radio, as opposed to shouting on the radio, which was something I used to do quite often: "It's NOT the North Sea! It's the North Atlantic."

West of Shetland, north-west of where I live, where The Last Bookshop sits, the tragedy of the *Bourbon Dolphin* had been unfolding, and basic geography was being ignored in the journalistic search for poignancy and colour. Geography which was crucial to the terrible events which had happened in 3600 feet of water, in a marine environment much more demanding than the North Sea. Everyone was getting it wrong – reporters, sub editors, editors.

Next morning I was shouting at newspapers, or rather, shouting about them. Again, right up the chain of editorial command went that simplest of errors: if it's an oil rig and it's off Shetland, it must be in the North Sea. After all, that's where the oil is, isn't it?

And they will have looked at maps, those reporters, putting agency copy together on their computers. There's always a map of Scotland lurking, usually out of date, almost always with Shetland in a box, somewhere right of Inverness. My friend, the photographer Stewart Cunningham, told me of a major argument he had with a London picture editor who wanted him to 'nip over to the Shetlands' for a job.

"Do you realise how far that is?" asked Clydebank-based Stewart. "It's an overnight ferry crossing."

"It can't be," came the metropolitan reply. "I'm looking at a map, and the Shetlands are in the Moray Firth."

William Goldman, the Hollywood scriptwriter (*Butch Cassidy and the Sundance Kid, Marathon Man* etc) has a variety of pithy sayings, including the infamous 'Nobody Knows Anything'. But in one of his books, he argues that all journalism, documentary film making (and, obviously, fictional treatments of 'real' events) will be, to an expert or anyone who has local knowledge, wrong. This is partly down to the journalist's need to summarise, cut to the chase, make the facts fit the tale or, more likely, the available space. For the journalist (and this was not always the case) a missing or inaccurate detail does not affect the thrust of the story. For the reader, it compromises the entire thing.

How do you trust a journalist who thinks that facts don't matter. How do you trust their tale? In some long ago coverage concerning the alleged sexual misdemeanours of SNP MP Aonghas-Ethelred NicGedhachaearn, it took a week to correct the erroneous report that his supposed 'three in a bed romp' (with accompanying comatose and presumably oblivious piper in an armchair) had taken place during the Island Games in Shetland. Instead, it happened in Orkney at a completely different time. But hey, that doesn't matter, shrugs the reporter. The story's the thing.

Ah yes, the tale, the story. What was the 'story' in the tragic capsize of the *Bourbon Dolphin*? National newsdesk values would dictate that it was quite simple: eight are killed when an almost new, Norwegian oil supply vessel capsizes while engaged in anchor handling 75 miles north west of Shetland. Seven escape.

No, that's not the 'story'. There are several narratives here: there is the miraculous escape of seven men. The tragic death of eight others. The desperate search for survivors. The grief of a tiny Norwegian community. But more emotionally potent than anything else was the (presumed) drowning of the 14-year-old son of the skipper (the captain was pulled from the water in the initial rescue, but did not survive). Any of us with children could feel the stabbing at the heart, the horror of a mother imagining how her son and husband had died.

And that became the story. At this time in this culture, we seem to be incapable of absorbing facts. Sober, straightforward reporting is not enough. We are immune to their power. We need pictures, preferably moving, preferably intimate, possibly horrific. And if we are to have words, mere words, they have to clutch us by the throat and shake us, evoke tears, empathy. Or we don't get it. Our sensitivities have become blunted, so that we, it seems, need the histrionic effects of 'colour' before we can understand what has happened. It's like only being able to understand sex by using pornography.

Tell me, what could be more powerful than this, reprinted from the professional journal *The Shipping Times*:

Missing: David Remøy (14), Herøy – the Captain's son who was on work experience,
Frank Nygård (42), Hareid – Chief Engineer,
Ronny Emblem (25), Ålesund – Second Engineer,
Søren Kroer (27), Ørum Djurs, Denmark – Electrician,
Tor Karl Sandø (54), Ålesund – Bosun.
Confirmed dead:
Bjarte Grimstad (37), Hareid – Chief Officer,
Kjetil Rune Våge (31), Ålesund (originally from Sande) – Second Officer.

Seven men were rescued alive.

Yes, I plead guilty to some terrible, self-seeking, emotion-wringing 'journalism' in the past. I have waded in wholesale, notebook swinging, where sensitivity was required. I have abused hospitality, invaded privacy, streamlined quotes, threatened and personalised. I have been careless and inaccurate. And yes, maybe I still am. Quidawick and Ramnavine are places it may be difficult to find on a map.

I wrote most of the above in a fit of sad rage, 10 years ago. Now we appear to be living in a post-factual world, where evidence and truth do not matter, out-Trumped by emotion and bluster; by sheer noise. Social media is not the cause of this, but its sheer immediacy and lack of editing, lack of curation, encourages the relaying of half- and untruth, the lurid and the lie.

And I wanted to write about someone I knew, played music

with, who died, tragically when the fishing boat he was on sank in stupid, unnecessary circumstances. But I can't. I'm sorry, I just can't..

Walk

Shetland is Very Far Away. A minimum 12 hours by sea from Aberdeen, more if you go via Orkney or are smitten by God in a force-11 bad mood and heaving-to becomes necessary (in addition to the more personal kind of heaving, which is compulsory). You could of course fly, but this may involve mortgaging several houses and a level of fear novel to travellers more used to, say, Nemesis at Alton Towers or freefall parachuting into Helmand Province. It's a difficult choice: on the Shetland flight, you think you're going to die; on the boat, you wish you were dead.

Not always. Sometimes it's calm. You can occasionally persuade FlyBe to transport you for less than half your annual income. But still. Once you land at Sumburgh or wobble down that Lerwick gangplank you ain't in Kansas anymore. Or, for that matter, in Scotland. Not really.

I live here, and grow increasingly reluctant to leave. It's not the Scandinavian welfare-state economy, fuelled by the biggest oil terminal in Europe. It's not the low unemployment, the wealth, the state-of-the-art sports centres, state-of-the-sport arts centres, fabulous education system and ubiquity of that fine vehicle, the Toyota HiLux Double Cab pickup. It's not the nightless summers or the blink-and-you'll-miss-it daylight of winter. It's not the fiddle music or the reestit mutton soup. It's being Very Far Away.

There is, however, the issue of islanditis, that nervy sense of insularity that can descend, even in the endless days of the simmer dim. If it's not a sudden desire for multiplexes and Eggs Benedict, it's a yearning for proper hills, decent trees and an absence of sea. And then, as the summer begins to expire, you sense the

91

encroaching blackness and wish you had actually gone on those wee treks you promised yourself. This year, last year, the year before that. In particular, the Big One, the perambulation par excellence. The Best Beaches in the World Walk.

As you may be aware, there are other candidates in The Best Beaches in the World category. Upstarts such as Bondi, Sandwood Bay, Copacabana, Nairn. Forget all that. The best beaches of the world are all in Shetland. The South Mainland has the golden fineness of Spiggie, Boddam and especially the stunning tombolo, or double-sided beach, at St Ninian's Isle (which possesses flattened pebbles so wondrous I once considered selling them on eBay in packs of four to aid meditation). The East and West Ayres at Quidawick have their charms, but things get really interesting when you hit the red granite that gives the northern part of the North Mainland its various names: North Redskerry, Hjalda Hill, Roer Water. Ro, Roer, Ronas. Red, red, red. Hidden away beneath some of the fractured, cave-pocked cliffs of Karaness lie gritty shingle strands, only reachable via dodgy scrambles down ever-shifting watercourses for which you should really bring ropes, helmets and years of experience. But, in my case, never do. Fear of the embarrassment which would be involved in calling out the local coastguard, every man and woman of which is a friend or neighbour, mean that you simply cannot get stuck, get hurt or go missing. It is Not Allowed.

The two best beaches in Shetland – or, let's be fair, my favourites – and hence in the world, are the Muckle Ayre (big beach) and the small tombolo at Urad Isle. The Muckle Ayre can be reached only be sea or by a long walk either over the top of Hjalda Hill, Shetland's highest peak, or along its Specially Scientifically Interesting flank. Urad Isle lies about six miles to the north of the Muckle Ayre. Urad itself is an old crofting township, now inhabited only during the lambing season but containing some of the most fertile land in Shetland. There's a drivable track from Redskerry, grant-aid widened in places to almost motorway dimensions. It corkscrews through the Beorgs of Urad and past such wondrous Norse nomenclature as Heogel of the Moor and Moosa Breck. No

Gaelic here. Urad, when reached from this route, appears like a green mirage, truly magnificent, a kind of scoured Shangri-La with extra sleet.

The summer was fading, and my ambition was to walk from the old NATO station at Vronnafirth Hill across Hjalda Hill, down to the Muckle Ayre, and, as instructed by Squadron Leader Roger Mann author of *Tramping the Coastline of Shetland*, camp at Muckle Clodie Wick. Then a morning's walk to Urad and out by the track, there to be collected at the Redskerry phonebox. It's 20 very rough and totally isolated miles. No mobile phone signal, once you're out of sight of the Vronnafirth masts. There are hidden drops, pits and bogs. And if the weather gets frisky, you don't want to be there. This is home to the UK's highest windspeeds: a gust of over 173mph was recorded at Muckle Flugga lighthouse on 1 January 1992, before the equipment broke. Two tourists were killed in that storm when the hut they were staying in blew away. In 1962, 177mph was recorded at the radar dome on top of Saxa Vord in Unst – and then the apparatus was ripped apart. The official UK record remains 173mph on Cairngorm in 1986; their equipment seems to be more solidly anchored.

Anyway. You really don't want to be walking "da banks" of the Muckle Ayre any time between October and February, and you most certainly don't want to be camping. Even in summer, weather is an obsession for Shetlanders. And, in this case, for me – a soothmoother, someone who arrived through the South Mouth of Lerwick Harbour.

As it happened, the forecast was for dullness, dreichocity and saturation, but not excessive blowing. And so Saturday lunchtime saw me dropped off at Vronnafirth by my son, who thinks I am mad. I certainly look mad, rucksacked-up with a Quechua one-man pop-up tent, light enough at two kilos but in its ineffable, green circularity making me look like a middle-aged Mutant Turtle.

The walk from the masts at Vronnafirth Hill to the top of Hjalda Hill took about two hours. This scarred granite bounder field is often compared to the sub-arctic tundra of northern Norway. The existence of a Neolithic chambered cairn (somewhat modified since the 1960s, but still very impressive), 40 metres below at the summit, never fails to give me the creeps, especially if up here in mist. Trowies (Shetlandic troll-Picts) infest the corners of your eyes. Still, it's worth squirming in to see if the 'ritual objects' that occasionally appear here have been nicked. Confront the creepiness!

Onwards, though, to The Best Beach in Britain. And the Muckle Ayre, when reached, viewed from the Stonga Banks or after an occasionally intimidating scramble down the smashed granite course of the Burn of Monius, was truly breathtaking. A mile-and-a-half of red shingle, backed with cliffs that give every impression of imminent crumbling. There are caves, infinite amounts of scran (beachcombing assets) and, offshore, the monstrous gothic-perpendicular stacks of the Cleiver and the Hog. Now there was a choice. To trudge along the strength-sapping shingle and trust the (surely no longer safe) standing rope at Turls Head to get back to the clifftop. Or scramble back up the burn. Long-left ropes attached to dubious spikes don't appeal to me. I only knew about the rope (I couldn't find it from the top) because a far fitter friend, walking alone, used it a couple of years ago, despite a halfway-up panic attack. Hereabouts, though, as a Karaness pal is fond of saying about his home, there's nobody to hear you scream.

Onwards, as another mile of beach-scimitar curves below the Valla Kames. There are some treacherous fissures and bottomless holes hereabouts, but the ground is largely firm. Inland, there are dozens of small lochs and some very mire-ridden sections on the short route out to the reservoir at Roer Water; at Muckle Clodie Wick, where all the available water empties itself down two of the most spectacular waterfalls in Shetland, the short springy heather and rocky outcrops surrounding the death-black loch provide a dry and sheltered spot for camping. Indeed, it's probably the best camping location in the whole of Shetland. There's fresh water, shelter, astonishing views. There's also a truly odd, stone-lined and slab-roofed pit which Squadron Leader Mann ruminates may be all that remains of a "a Neolithic motel". But it was too early to stop, really, so I pressed on. I'm not afraid of ghosts. Honest.

On Hevdadale Hill, after an almost total absence of both fences and sheep, both began to make their presence felt. The Woolly Gods were back. I was getting sore and hungry, and though I could have pressed on and camped on the flatlands of Uyea, I opted for the amazing little canyon through which the Burn of Brettoo reaches the Red Geo, just along from Tongan Swarta. Feet washed in the fast-flowing, brutally cold water, I established my temporary home. The tent popped up and properly pegged out (who ever knows what the wind will do?), the Trangia was lit and, for a couple of hours before the sun drifted slowly into the north Atlantic, I entered that meditative state of pleasantly uncomfortable knackeredness that is solo overnighting. Old Pulteney 12 helped: a salty, outdoors whisky if ever there was one.

Curious sheep disturbed me during the short night. In the utter darkness the stars arced, massive and soft, haloed like Christmas decorations. I got up in dampish, billowing weather and packed quickly. Bad rain was fluttering in the air.

Signs of cultivation and modern crofting increased: quad-bike tracks, new fences. But there was not a soul around as I reached Urad and trekked for what seemed like miles across the runway-like pasture to the isle itself. The morning was closing in fast: grey, cold, wet. The tombolo joining the island to the mainland is tiny compared to the huge strand at St Ninian's Isle, but it's a jewel. Second-best Beach in Britain? There are stories of Dutch East Indiaman gold in that sand, just as there are horrid tales of pirate murders just a bit north towards Sandvoe. There is one campsite the superstitious should avoid, where one buccaneer was buried alive, leaving only his head exposed to the predatory bonxies.

The climb out of Urad on the track (suitable for 4x4s, but get permission first; access is always open for walkers and mountain bikers) seemed endless. As the road veered in and out of the Beorgs of Urad, the cairns showing the site of a Neolithic axe factory were visible on the skyline. I was too tired and my ancient knees were too creaky to attempt the climb, but I wondered if there were any axe heads left. My wife claims to have seen dozens when she was last here 20 years ago, and items quarried here have been found all over Europe.

Redskerry, finally. Still no mobile-phone signal, and the red phonebox is a mile along the main road from the track-end, next to the sadly closed shop. By the time I get there, icy rain is pummelling down, sideways and around, in the classic Shetland fashion. I call Susan. She'll be here in 20 minutes.

Squatting on my rucksack, I read the Squadron Leader's quotation of his fellow RAF man, Derek Gilpin Barnes, stationed at RAF Sullom Voe during World War Two and a keen explorer of the local landscape: "Did the brooding spirits of the ancient gods whisper to my companions as they did to me? Was that thin silence shattered in the quiet of their minds, by the clash of remote Scandinavian swords or the grinding of Norse keels upon those forgotten sands?"

Or is that the rattle of a Toyota Landcruiser's turbo diesel, coming to whisk me home for the winter? Not very far away at all. By car.

Seahouse

Sand bags are not bags of sand, not in this neck of the bog. They are bags of grit, bags of gravel, sacks of small stones. Sand, sharp sand, builder's sand? That would wash away, like the beaches sometimes do, sucked in and spat out by the biggest tides, wiped out by the wind.

The council has supplied us with gritbags, stonebags, gravelbags, and they are piled around the front door like the clusters of dead sheep you sometimes see, huddled against snowdrifted walls, revealed by the thaw. We wait.

We wait for the top of the tide. We wait for the flood.

We've done our best with this 300-year-old former Church of Scotland manse. The massive rock armouring along the shoreline was diggered in after the last major flood, in the late 1970s, when seawater was lapping a foot from the Rayburn's top, according to Fitchin, who was there, bailing, perched atop the stove with a bucket. The big stone house crouches on a beach, a shingle peninsula, just six metres or so from high water mark. And these days, the highest of high tides, the springs, are level with our doorstep on a calm day. So we have built extra walls, channels, drains and runnels to deal with the malevolent storm surges that come with a couple of days of big Atlantic swells, building far out in the ocean and a wind of a particular, vicious bent. A westerly's the one to watch for, when it starts backing, and great slurping, sloshing surges begin walloping around the bay. That's when you're looking at trouble. Or at night, listening for it, waiting.

The cast-iron Rayburn stove is a religion, surrounded by ritual, fear, hope, faith, deliverance, eternal hellfire. We burn peat, cut from our own banks. Sustainable? Probably not, not over 100,000 of your earth years, but more so than the Government-subsidised wood that is now fashionable and cheap on this treeless archipelago. Peat is local, hand-harvested over a backbreaking spring and summer. Peat is history. I'm thinking of Gunnister man, the 18th-century traveller found in mummified near perfection by cutters just a mile or two away. I'm thinking of 'blue' peat, the coal-like treasure that burns quickly and very hot, and the wet slabs of turf used to damp a fire that threatens to run out of control. Peat tar coats chimneys and if the lum catches, usually on a windy night, it's like some kind of nuclear inferno that can, and does, melt stone.

This third-hand Rayburn, a Series 1 Landrover to a suburban Aga's Range Rover Vogue, can be fine-tuned to handle the worst storm in the world. We've learned how to deal with it, finally, after hard, costly lessons involving the fire brigade, disastrous and dangerous sweeping attempts and leaking water jackets. Now, it's hurricane proof. All flaps are closed. It's our servant, not our flue-destroying master. Chim Chim Cheree! Water is croaking and bubbling in the backboilers, up the copper pipes to the radiators we bought from the old Rogerhead Prison.

Tonight, it feels like the worst storm in the world is with us. But then, it often feels that way. In the downstairs toilet, the WC is waterless, the wind creating low pressure that sucks it dry. I pour a bucket down, for emergencies. It disappears in seconds.

It's been dark since 2.35pm. There will be a brief flicker of low, oppressive daylight around 9.30am. Or maybe tomorrow will never lighten beyond a kind of permanent dusk. Whatever, we're in proper, northern winter darkness, the TV up high so it's audible above the storm. Blink. Blackness. Bleeping from the uninterruptible power supplies I use to keep the broadcasting and computer gear going if I'm on air, giving me time to get the generator, going, out in the washhouse. It's a Honda. I've never bought anything but Honda outboards and generators since a terrifying chase after a boat that had snapped its mooring, and was being sent lurching furiously towards Iceland by a nasty wee squall. I jumped from the pursuing salmon farm tender into my beloved

Shetland Model, and said a prayer to Soichiro-San that his, and my three-year old outboard motor would start. It did.

This is now a west-south-westerly force 11, gusting higher. Towards 100 mph or so, too high and from the west, so getting to the washhouse through the porch's sliding door is dangerous, maybe impossible. Time to check the candles, torches, make a last cup of tea from Rayburn-boiled water. All switches off, the stove tamped right down. Check the phone – still working. Susan, a GP, is on call for emergencies, 24-hours availability. NHS Direct? Be Serious. A final prayer for no call-outs, and so to bed amid the groaning, muttering, howling and rattling of this old, old house. The windows are solid, double glazed, built by a local firm from (sustainable) hardwood. When they were fitted, when the old ones were removed, the original frames were revealed as recycled ship's spars, complete with adze-marks and cleats. The beams under the kitchen slabs are pitch pine, 300 years old or more, and when they were cut for central heating pipes the smell of sap was as fresh as Domestos.

The phone doesn't ring. We sleep sound and unmoving. Gunnister Man and Woman. It's the silence that wakes us.

Late, veering towards nine, the first dark blue signifier of morning, the wind, the sky, the world has dropped. As the atmospheric pressure has lifted, the sense of oppression, of greater gravity has increased. The air is jellied, thick, all movement is slow and sluggish. And the world has changed. Things have shifted, been rearranged, like God playing stroppily with someone else's Lego. Everything has been slowed and stunned by the violence of the storm

By 10.30, you can see, dimly, through windows frosted with salt. The grass is covered with shingle and stones. Susan's car has a smashed quarterlight – the Landcruiser's interior is all glass and shingle. The peat stack has been levelled, scattered, and there is wave-borne bruck right up to the front door. Tangle and kelp everywhere. It's like the ocean has been on some almighty bender, has vomited its guts out. Now it needs to sleep. Until the next time. There's a menacing stillness to the waveless water of Quida Wick

There is seaweed all around the washhouse door. But the Sea House is still standing, just as it always has, as it probably always will. I pull on the Honda's starting cord, and the building bursts into life.

Thule

They say the Thule folk don't sleep at this time of year.

Summer above 60 degrees of latitude. The light never entirely disappears, not even in the grimmest depths of night. An eternal, glimmering dawn, a constant sunset. Simmer Dim, in local dialect, the summer twilight.

But from 5.00am, even on days when cloud sweeps down or the evaporating sea turns mysteriously into cold, clammy, all enveloping mist, the light won't let me sleep. Pearly or harsh, hard-shadowed or woozy and buttery, no curtain can keep it out. It turns dreams to wakeful speculation, blurs the difference between nightmare and fact. And I have to get up. I have somewhere to go. But not Thule.

Thule is a tiny island 15 miles west of Shetland; hard, angular, jutting angrily from the sea. It looks resentful. Its harsh silhouette seems strangely familiar the first time you see it, and you may find swelling orchestral music and the jerky movements of camp puppetry swimming into your head. The Tracey Family. Brains. The Evil Hood. *Thunderbirds Are Go*. It was Thule's sinister shape that allegedly inspired Tracey island, though this North Atlantic outpost has no palm trees, no swimming pool, no luxury hideaway. It's famed for its seabirds, the quality of its seaweed fed lamb, and the fact that 30 or so people live there, doing, it seems very little.

Except, some Shetlanders will mutter, claiming subsidies and moaning, About their ferry, on which many islanders have jobs, and for a while was always breaking down. About their harbour, which is so exposed boats have to be lifted out of the water if the wind rises beyond a whisper. About their complicated renewable power

101

scheme, installed at a cost of millions, which uses hydro-electric and wind power to provide electricity, and is always breaking down. About their school which periodically closes down because there are no pupils.

The stories: was it true that Thule folk hibernated in the winter, never slept in the summer, never bothered going to bed? If so, what do they do during the endless outpouring of ultra-violet light? The famous Thule sheep (and nothing, nothing tastes better than lean, seaweed-fed Thule lamb; other than possibly Thule mutton) need little or no looking after. There are only so many shags (small members of the cormorant family, not roving embodiments of illicit sex) that can be shot (this is illegal but a long-rumoured aspect of Thule's Christmas celebrations. And when I say Christmas I mean Yule. And when I say 'Yule' I mean Old Yule, Aald Jül, because the Thule folk sort of adhere to the Julian calendar, which celebrates Christmas/Yule/Jül on 6 January).

What do Thule folk do? They keep sheep, and ponies. They enjoy the island's soaring boglands; they may occasionally climb the Kame, the highest sheer sea cliff in the UK, to gaze out at... the sea. They explore the mysterious remains of World War Two aircraft, left to moulder on the island's interior wastes. If I lived there, that's what I'd do. I'd sit and think in the winter. And possibly drink. And search the skies for the daily plane from Tingwall, hustling in to the clifftop, mud-and-grass airstrip.

Summer, though. Maybe, like me, they just can't sleep. Maybe they get out of bed, clean up the mess left by an aged, incontinent dog, switch on the radio and dream of living somewhere, anywhere else. And then they settle down to the day, the everlasting summer day, and gradually the island takes them over, soothes, hypnotises. Something, maybe home brew, maybe the promise of an imminent council subsidy, a fiddle tune, the coming of the weekly ferry with a selection of eBay orders... *something* gets them through the endless hours. Or perhaps the thought of winter, looming, inevitable, when the northern darkness descends and you can sleep, sleep all through the day light hours and the blessed blackness of night.

I have been to Thule. I liked it. The people were shy, but

essentially friendly. The island is not a pristine tourist destination, or a National Trust-controlled park like Fair Isle. It's a mess, awash with rusty cars and dead tractors. I have never been there in the depths of January, when daylight is a brief flicker in Shetland, a kind of lazy blink. But when they're not sleeping, I know the locals have winter fire ceremonies, very different from the gentrified delights of Up Helly Aa, when the worst of the still-mobile cars are doused in petrol and, flaming, sent spiralling over the cliffs and into the sea.

The shag hunt, too, is a winter institution. They pretend to keep to the Julian calendar, but actually run to both, celebrating two Christmases, Two Yules, Two New Years. There are age-old feuds, an extended and fractured family of the original lairds, resentments, half-buried scandals, and lovely charming folk as well as strange figures in peaty beards and bloated wellies. And people who nobody knows anything about, who are rarely seen, who don't speak. Who arrived mysteriously and may not even be there anymore.

Really, it's just like anywhere else.

Maybe they do sleep more in the winter. I know I do. In fact, sometimes, summer mind battered by yet another incandescent 4.00am dawn, I long for the brutal shrieking winds, the slashing windchill, the enveloping eternal darkness of winter. Sleep. Oh, sleep!

The tininess and remoteness of the island simply exaggerates the eddies and currents which run through every community, and make them more visible. More the stuff of legend for observers and visitors.

Thule is what we, on the Mainland of Shetland, fear we'll become. It's what we fear we already are.

***   ***   ***

I'm thinking about pigs. Pigs and Thule are inextricably linked for me, because back in our years of fantasy crofting (the Bible: John Seymour's amazing book *Self-Sufficiency*) we sent our most

103

beloved pig to Thule, there to see out his last days with one of the island's legends, a woman I shall call Angela. The funny thing is that 'gone to Thule' is a phrase commonly used on mainland Shetland to disguise, for a child's sake, the fact that an animal (pig, dog, horse, caddie lamb (pet sheep)) has died. Where's Ertie the Gloucester old Spot? Gaan ta Thule, comes the reply, through munched pork crackling. Our pig, though, Derek the Randy Boar, did really go to Thule. He happily saw out the remainder of his existence there, successfully (and for the first time in his somewhat unrampant life) impregnating a sow. He must have been, well, bored. Animals can't resort to home brew, shag shooting or long hours of subsidy-claim-form filling to occupy the weary hours.

Derek was supposedly a pedigree 'kune-kune' pig, a new Zealand breed that has become favoured in recent years among smallholders, for no earthly reason I can think of. It's black, hairy and the boar tends to grow enormous tusks, if you don't extract them during babyhood (pliers, no anaesthetic, horrendous child-like screams; I really don't recommend it. Nor do I recommend piglet castration, which is like shelling peas, only again with screams and squirming. They do taste good fried, though, the ah, sweetbreads. Garlic, olive oil, a little salt).

The truth is that some kune-kunes brought into the UK have become interbred with wild boar, which are not really wild boar, but tame boar reared for their meat and allowed to escape, so that they become wild. Wildened Boar, if you see what I mean. Then the wild boar break back into the pens of the expensive kune-kunes and get jiggy with the sows. The end result is an advert in *Smallholder Magazine* or on the internet for surprisingly cheap 'pure' bred kune-kunes, which are sometimes bought by escapees form the urban pig race, who scoop up the bargain swine in their new Land Rover Defenders and take them to their remote crofts, Very Far Away. People like us, in fact, or to be precise, people like Dougal.

Dougal has been everywhere, done it all. He has beach-shacked in Thailand, rented out windsurfing equipment in Albania. He has travelled the Silk Road, smoked dope in Afghanistan (before the war), squatted with dodgy jazz rock bands in Colchester and Wick.

Or so he says. Actually, I think he probably has done all those things. For a few weeks, maybe months. Until he got bored and moved on. Or until everyone in the vicinity got fed up coping with him and politely asked him to leave.

Dougal is alone, these days, in Ramnavine, on his croft called Bökkra, though he is extremely, if politely and non-physically, flirtatious at hall dances and socials. Everyone likes him. Everybody knows about his criminal record for growing and selling dope down in Cornwall – it's on Google – but if he does that these days, it's for personal use only. There are rumours of wives, one or two families, though none have ever turned up here. He has some money. Quite a lot, but doesn't revel in it. Everybody likes Dougal.

However, living with him as a neighbour (and he's far enough way not be classed as such in our case, thank God) is a nightmare of half-completed projects, escaped horses (during his Shetland pony-and-trap riding school period), three bulls (a venture into the provision of a sperm bank for local cattle) and, to the consternation of many, a snail farm which saw, during a brief spurt of fine summer weather, a kind of slow-motion breakout of edible gastropods covering an unbelievable and very slimy 20 square miles. Fortunately, the herring gulls, skuas great and small, kittiwakes and gulls generally made short work of the roaming escargots.

And then there were the pigs.

The pigs arrived after a trip south by Dougal in his Type Two Landrover, towing a disreputable home-made stock trailer full of carefully clingfilmed peat, cut for sale, block by block, at a farmer's market near Truro.

"Do people from Truro even know what peat is?" He'd asked me to help load the trailer before he left, and I was more than slightly concerned.

"It's like a whiff of the islands, if you put it on a fire or in a cooker. Like coffee beans, when you're selling a house," he replied. "That welcoming aroma. Or whisky."

I pondered the awful peat reek you got in Shetland crofthouses, the phenolic fog that could render a 20-a-day smoker helpless with racking splutters.

"But does anybody have any notion of what burning peat smells like, down in Cornwall?" I thought about Dartmoor's boggy wastes. Maybe they had peat there. Maybe, in the past, before Rick Stein and Damien Hirst, before tin, pasties and ice cream, before they ate tourists, the Cornish religiously cut it, took it home and heated their houses with it, just as people in Shetland still do. Despite the killing work involved – 16 different human interventions, someone once calculated, from hill to fireplace – and sneaky worries about global warming, dirty hands and midge attack. "And isn't the place full of hippy environmentalists who think peat bogs should be left in peace, like the Amazon rain forest? Stop the Carbon, all that stuff?"

Dougal stopped loading his cling-filmed briquettes (none too solidly made or wrapped, they were crumbling already).

"Souvenirs," he said, thoughtfully. "In Ireland, they export bits of peat to America. People put them on their mantelpieces and dream about their native land. Or their great grandfather's native land. Ould Sod, it's called. They make millions."

"How many Shetlanders are there in Cornwall?"

"Race memory," he said. "The Celtic commonality. Not all Cornish folk are conceptual artists, you know. Or cooks."

I shrugged and shut up.

In the end, and amazingly, he sold the peat, at a more-than-knockdown (just) price, to none other than a cook, the experimental 'scientific' chef, a disciple of that bald, alien skiddler Heston Blumenthal, called Ciaran Hoffsetter. He wanted to use it for the infusion of ice cream or somesuch. And Dougal spent the money on three kune-kune pigs. From a man he met in a pub.

Kune-kunes are originally from New Zealand. They're supposed to be descended from a Maori breed, examples of which, in that classic native village way, were left running loose to scavenge around local houses, eat shit, much of it their own, and dig up the ground like organic excavators. They're fond of humans (for company, not food, though like all swine they will eat anything, including human flesh if it falls down dead of a heart attack in front of them; be warned). They're hairy, have two little dangly tassels called piri-piri hanging from their chins, and they're small. They're comedy pigs, really, like the once-trendy Vietnamese pot-bellied, only with hair. George Clooney probably has a couple. There were only 18 kune-kunes left in New Zealand in 1976, when two guys called Michael Willis and John Simister started breeding the things and then selling them to self-sufficiency freaks throughout the world.

Anyway. Dougal arrived back in Shetland with the islands' first kune-kunes. and, God help us, we bought two of them. A boar and a sow.

As I say, this was during our fantasy crofting years. It was our first venture into pigdom. Two wee pigs, we thought, charming and hairy. The children will adore them. We'll breed them, sell some piglets, feed up the remaining ones, eat them. Make our own bacon. And later, much later, we would do that. But not with the two kune kunes which we named Derek and Matilda. The small pigs which grew, and grew, bigger and bigger, until each was the size of a small tractor. The friendly pigs who were, respectively, suicidal and grumpy. The ones that grew tusks, were resolutely black when they should have been mottled, and began to look more and more like the wild boar-kune-kune crosses the vet said they were.

There are herds of wild boar in Cornwall, apparently, roaming the countryside like vengeful packs of tusk-toting, evil spirits. They are escapees from boar-farming projects, aimed at satisfying Cornish superchefs' desire for exotic meats to feed, raw and bleeding, to their idiot customers. They attack hippy small holdings and impregnate kune-kunes, pot-bellied Gloucester Old Spots and probably horses for all I know (the wild boar, not the chefs). The resultant mongrel animals are then flogged to hapless visiting would-be peat entrepreneurs in pubs.

Matilda, carrying no doubt some deep seated complex derived from her wild boar past (boredom, possibly) and transplantation from the balmier climes of New Zealand, committed suicide, Legion style, by escaping from her pen and wandering off a cliff. This is always a possibility in Shetland where cliffs abound. In the old days, before playpens and electric fences, children were often tethered to posts to stop them doing the same thing. That left us Derek.

We could have killed and eaten him. The kids probably wouldn't have minded. Our youngest was then a dribbling blob and the oldest, at six or thereabouts, had a hard-eyed curiosity about such things. But Derek, as pigs, even kune-kune/wild boars of uncertain pedigree, do, had developed a personality. He was the Victor Meldrew of swinedom. He was cussed, he was sour. He was the grumpiest pig who ever existed. And somehow, you had to respect that.

Pigs are supposed to be, at least physically, more like beings than any other creature alive. That's why pig hearts are used for transplants. And presumably pig souls too. They get colds. Their giant snouts run with snot. You wipe their noses, and even, when the sun shines too much, slather them with factor 30. This became an issue with Derek, as his hair began to fall out soon after Matilda's self-termination.

He needed companionship. He wasn't going to get any on the Dougal front, as his own sow had been, with some alacrity, sold on to an acquaintance of his on Thule, Angela. She was a former professor of women's studies from Tonbridge in Kent who had abandoned everything to move to Thule and write. And, it should be said, take up with a tattooed Norwegian ex-mercenary. But that's another story.

So Derek went to Thule. He was, snuffling and grunting in annoyance, tempted onto a stock trailer by a bucket of mashed tatties with garlic butter (his favourite), and then, igmoniously crated up and craned onto the ferry, the *Westering*, commonly known as the *Festering*. We never saw him again, but every month or so Angela would telephone, always late at night, with news of his progress. He thrived in Thule. He fathered several piglets. (By this time, we had realised that Matilda and the other sow were probably his sisters, but that was the Pig Fact That Dare Not Speak Its Name) and Angela (as well as Thor, her some time AK47-toting partner) was very fond of Derek.

He passed away from complications involving the eating of a

football. Angela was upset. So were we, a bit. So, presumably, was the child whose leather football, a Christmas present, had been kicked into Derek's pen. Getting a replacement on Thule couldn't have been straightforward. Unless they simply decapitated Derek and used his head, or possibly, to keep with tradition, his tanned and inflated stomach. One doesn't really like to think of such things. But the stories they tell about Thule sometimes make you wonder...

Like this business of them hibernating in winter and staying awake summer. It can't be true. But right now, as the sun climbs higher and the dusky half-dawn of the simmer dim floods into full daytime, I wonder. I can't sleep. I'm like Al Pacino in that movie *White Nights*, insomniac in Alaska, befuddled, seeking a murderer, murdering...

No, actually, I'm not. I'm just here in the light, yearning for the darkness. In the treeless peatscape, wishing I could hear the swish of a forest, not the click and hiss of waves on stones. I'm thinking about the dusty, exhaust-fume-laden, oily atmosphere of a city, the rush and whirl of cars and crowds. I'm longing not to be the lone figure in this empty landscape, desperate for the taste of commercial cappuccino, urban curry.

It'll pass, the feeling they call soothlag. It always does. It's something to do with the summer.

Questions

What, you mean *The Shetlands*?

No. It's not and never has been and never is *The Shetlands*. Despite what that Botoxed TV newsreader said five minutes ago. Despite what it says in your newspaper, magazine, dictionary or that guy you met down the pub who says he used to work in the North Sea oil industry. It's not 'The Shetlands'. It's 'Shetland', singular.

It's singular in Norse (Hjaltland), Faroese (Hetland) and 'Shetland' is simply a phonetic transliteration taken from a drunk Norseman with no teeth by an even drunker Scot with a shaky quill. 'Hjalt' and 'Het' both mean the hilt or cross guard of a sword, which is kind of the archipelago's shape and captures the place's geographical importance in terms of warlike raiding of the (much more fertile and lucrative) bits of land to the south.

From a Celtic southerner's point of view, that is to say, in Gaelic, the uncivilised lumps of rock north of Orkney were known as Inse Catt, 'Islands of the Cat People', which simply goes to show that the late David Bowie's least creative period was a lot earlier than anyone suspected. Putting out fire with gasoline, indeed.

Ahem. 'Cat People' would be a reference to the nasty wee hairy Picts who survived in Shetland longer than anywhere else, inside their upside-down stone-built flowerpot redoubts, the ones known as brochs. Until the vikings got round to wiping them out.

Incidentally, while research has proven that the Shetland population contains large quantities of Scandinavian genetic stuff, there is a theory that the Norsemen who stayed in (but not 'on'; you are never 'on The Shetlands'. You are 'in Shetland'.) Shetland were

110

rubbish vikings. They were the ones who whinged, the ones who got seasick, the ones who got ill, the ones nobody liked. The fearties who wanted off at the first landfall, or were unceremoniously dumped so the brave, fully-sea-legged-lads could go on their merry way, pillaging like crazy. The ones who stayed in Orkney were the farmers who saw all that fertile greensward and thought, och aye, this'll do. We shall establish a bourgeoisie!

But as I say, that's only a theory.

Where is Shetland?

It's in the sea, up from Scotland. No, it's further up than that, beyond Orkney, which is only a hop, skip and a jump off Caithness (which means 'Land of the Cat People'; there were hairy wee Picts there too). Keep going right a bit. There you are, that long scattering of over 100 different islands and islets, only 15 of which are actually inhabited by humans or their approximate relatives. You are In Shetland.

Distances? Well, which bit? From where? Let's settle for main sea port Lerwick – the capital, only town. Scalloway, which becomes more lovely with each passing year, is A Great Big Village but was, long ago, the capital. Grey, cluttered, and very similar at first sight to many superficially dreich places in north-eastern Scotland such as Rogerhead, Banff and Wick. All of which I like, actually, all of which have hidden attractions. Lerwick, of course, I love.

More than 100 miles from the nearest coast of mainland Scotland, about 210 miles north of Aberdeen, 230 miles west of Bergen in Norway, 230 miles (370 km) south east of Torshavn in the Faroe islands, where the natives eat whales, puffins but not for a long time, and then, only when really hungry, each other. You'll often hear people who should know better (notably, in a past life as a journalist, where inaccuracy is a way of life, me) saying that the nearest railway station to Lerwick is in Bergen. This is nonsense. The nearest railway station is in Thurso. True, it's not a very nice railway station, but parallel steel lines it most definitely possesses.

111

And trains occasionally run on them.

Does Shetland have any proper history?

Are you kidding? Shetland's got more history than you can shake a tushkar at (tushkar, similar to tuisgear in Gaelic: a tool used to cut peat). But basically, it comes down to this: Picts (wee hairy cat-like semi-human creatures – see above). Wiped out by vikings, mostly. One or two thought to survive at the back of Hjalda Hill. Possibly.

Up until the ninth century the vikings (Norwegian ones; the Danes tend to go further afield) are content to plunder. Then, as more and more of the weak, seasick and feartie vikings get left behind (one view) or shipwrecked vikings have to remain, or big strong, well-balanced and quite brave vikings fall for the undoubtedly-attractive local women and decide to stay, they decide they might as well just take over. So they do.

Fine. Shetland, and indeed, much of Scotland, including the Western isles, is overrun by big hairy vikings with axes, magic mushrooms and a tendency to decapitate monks. Then the barons fall out and there's around 300 years of general mayhem and malarkey between the kings and princes of Norway and various sulky lords based in Orkney and Shetland.

You can kind of see their point: "What, we've got to stay here when you've got everything from Bergen to the Arctic Circle to play with, possibly including the mysterious land of America Way Over There? Fight!"

And so to the 13th century, and all-out war between Alexander of Scotland and Haakon of Norway for control of Scotland. The Battle of Largs – no winners (sea battles tend to be like that – think of Jutland) but Haakon is over-extended and skulks back to Orkney, giving up Scotland and the Western isles. Nothing much happens for a couple of hundred years, and then comes the big event, the effects of which still reverberate down to Shetland today.

It's 1469, and the bankrupt king of Norway, Christian, needs to sort out a bit of a political stand-off by marrying off his daughter to William, King of Scots. There's no money for a dowry so, having already pawned Orkney to raise some gold, he does the same with Shetland. From this point on Shetland is essentially under Scots control, though the marriage never happens and there are frequent attempts right up until the 19th century to redeem the pledge with large lumps of currency. Still, that's it. Shetland becomes and remains Scottish, despite retaining a land tenure system and legal system based on Norse principles. Some today would like to claim that this means Shetland is not bound by British laws, and it is true that Udal Law still holds a certain sway on things like foreshore access and rights to driftwood. It was also deployed during a celebrated court case which came very close to denying the Crown Estate Commissioners authority over the seabed when it came to aquaculture. But not quite.

Anyway. Various Scottish lairdy folk grab Shetland (including an Earl of Morton, a Douglas from the Scottish border). Then there's famine, fishing (loads of herring then none), more famine, more fishing, two world wars (still the hilt of the sword, still strategic, full of soldiers and naval activity), the discovery of oil and everyone lives wealthily or not so wealthily, happily and unhappily ever after.

That, my friends, is the history of Shetland. Oh, and some radical socialists get obsessed by the romance of the vikings just after World War One, seeing them as symbolic of revolutionary freedom, and start a festival where everyone dresses up, has a party and burns a galley. That's called Up Helly Aa.

And that's another story altogether.

War

It's further north than Leningrad, on the same latitude as Anchorage, Alaska, perched on top of a hill called Saxa Vord, and far, far bigger than I ever imagined. There is a vast look-out pyramid, gazing sightlessly out to sea, towards the Muckle Flugga lighthouse which marks the northernmost end of Britain. Locked gates and still-secure fences glower at me; scary notices refer to the Official Secrets Act and the terrible fate that might befall you should you dare to break in. But everything is rusty, bedraggled and utterly deserted, and it's only as I slowly drive down the hill for a cup of coffee in Foord's Chocolate Shop and Cafe, known as the North Base, that I meet a lone, suspicious Land Rover hurtling upwards towards me.

There is just one RAF custodian left on the Shetland island of Unst (that's him in the Land Rover and the military hat), looking after what was once the first line of defence against Russian attack on the UK, the 'top and middle' bases of what was once RAF Saxa Vord. I pass muster – my old Volvo is quite recognisable – and with a wave I am descending, again, past sheep, peat banks and curious bonxies, great skuas, swooping like the F4 Phantoms and Tornado F3s that were once guided by the radar installations here against Russian bombers trespassing on British airspace. It's all a bit *Edge of Darkness*.

Down at Foord's there is a fascinating RAF museum full of pictures showing some of the social activities the several hundred men and their partners who lived and worked here from World War Two until the base's final, dwindled-down closure in 2006. The Saxa Vord dances, the Pelican Club – which sounds like something out of PG Wodehouse – the NAAFI and the bands formed by serving personnel are all legendary in Shetland. This was a difficult, wilderness posting and discipline was sympathetic, leisure taken very seriously. Not one, but two golf courses were constructed by the servicemen, remnants of one still being clearly visible at Burrafirth. And in the summer, the tradition of night golf in the 'simmer-dim', the midnight sun, began.

The hilltop radar base is maintained by the Ministry of Defence, reputedly with a view to reviving it as the threats from Vladimir Putin grow ever more strident. The main domestic base, along with the Nordabrake officers' accommodation, gym, football pitch and sergeants' mess, is now a holiday resort, complete with self-catering and hostel accommodation, bars, dining and more. It is known as the Saxa Vord Resort, which will amuse those RAF personnel who served here in the brutally brief, dark and stormy days of the Shetland winter. It is in the hamlet of Haroldswick, while further south, in Baltasound, Unst's main community, the Setter's Hill Estate of former RAF family units is now a mixture of public and privately-purchased housing.

The long-lost BBC Scotland TV comedy series *All Along the Watchtower* was reputedly based on Saxa Vord, and many are the tales still told today of goings-on at the base, over which I shall draw a discreet veil. There is, after all, the Official Secrets Act to think of.

Meanwhile, if you're planning a visit to Britain's Most Northerly... Everything, then may I recommend the drive up Saxa Vord and a lingering gaze at the way the Cold War was once fought. Remember, this beautiful and remote spot was once an official nuclear target for the Soviets. And, if you notice any activity at the site and a strange, new dome-like structure being erected, then, if you're thinking of settling down (property on Unst is cheap, as there's loads of it left over from the RAF days) remember: it still is.

Grave

November is the month of remembrance. Remembering the dead of not just two world wars, but the wars that have taken place since. The ones still going on. Those who left to serve and fight, but never returned. Shetland became a garrison in both world wars and, at the crossroads of the North Atlantic and the North Sea, a place familiar with the terrible cost of war. There were 78 recorded air crashes on or around Shetland in World War Two, many involving multiple fatalities.

And there were those given up by the sea. It's something rarely mentioned or discussed, and awful to contemplate – the many, many bodies washed ashore throughout Scotland in the course of World War One and World War Two. But a cursory look at headstones in coastal cemeteries throughout the country reveal the appalling numbers.

There are other signs of death and destruction still visible. On remote Shetland hilltops lie the remains of some of those 78 crashes. You can see the solidified remnants of heavy bunker oil from long-lost convoys ingrained in outcrops of rock, and until quite recently a bale of raw latex, cargo from a sunken cargo ship, was used to hold down hauled-up boats to the beach at Redskerry

But the gravestones all tell stories. Notably one in an ancient graveyard not far away from The Last Bookshop – the site of an ancient, now lost kirk, and near monastic settlements and signs of where a Pictish broch was ravaged for building stone. A place which has always been special, probably always holy, for as long as humans have been here.

The story of Petty Officer NE Lown centres on *HMS Bullen,* a

116

Captain class frigate built in the USA as part of the lend-lease scheme which saw a great deal of military matériel being provided for the use of British Forces in World War Two. She was system built as a submarine hunter, welded together like the notorious Liberty Ships, and her crew, probably including PO Lown, travelled to New York aboard the *Queen Mary* to bring her back across the Atlantic. They had some adventures in the USA, some of which you can hear about in the voice of one of the crew members, Rating John Albert Hodge, whose interviews are archived at the Imperial War Museum and online. The usual: nights on the town, much drinking, scuffles with the law. Young men on a spree.

HMS Bullen – named for one Nelson's commanders at the Battle of Trafalgar – joined the 19th Escort Group based at Belfast, and on 6 December 1944 she was off Cape Wrath, protecting a convoy which came under U-boat attack. But the submarine hunter became the hunted. A torpedo from *U-775*, commanded by Oberleutnant Erich Taschenmacher, hit her amidships and an explosion occurred on the starboard side, just behind the funnel. The aft engine room and boiler room probably flooded immediately. The ship quickly broke in two, the forepart turning on its beam ends and the aft-section floating vertically. Within an hour and six minutes, both parts of the ship had sunk. Ninety-seven men were rescued, many in a poor state from cold, injury or from inhaling oil. Seventy-two died. *U-775*'s part in the war was limited. She sank only the *Bullen* and one merchant ship. She was at sea on active service for a total of just 86 days.

Erich Taschenmacher survived the war, surrendering *U-775*, which was sunk by the Royal Navy along with dozens of other empty U-boats. *U-775* was used for target practice.

And Petty Officer Lown's body was taken by the sea, moved by the strange shifts of currents, eddies and tides, until it ended up in St Magnus Bay, to be buried in the company of Ramnamavine's dead, with other lost seamen, soldiers and civilians. In the strange hush of a round graveyard with its careful wall. But where the waves from the Atlantic can still be heard, and the beam of the Karaness lighthouse sweeps over each night like a blessing.

The heartbreaking family inscription, easily missed at the bottom of the stone, perhaps expresses the real cost of war, the true and eternal story of loss. And sums up why it is important that we remember, not just on 11 November, but always, the price that was paid by so many.

"To the world, he was just one. To me he was all the world. Always loved, deeply missed."

Hotel

Every night for four years or so I walked past the closed and shuttered St Rognvald Hotel and gazed longingly into the bar, scene of so much fun, fellowship, frolics and downright mayhem over the decades. Well, I didn't actually go up to the window and press my nose against the salt-encrusted glass. Not every night. Just occasionally. And I would weep for lost memories, for the ghosts who lurked within. And make sure none of those little dickheads who broke in and tried to light a bonfire in the bar had made any further amateurish attempts at arson.

The Hotel, always known as Ronnie's, had once provided Quidawick with, well, alcohol. And there were other Ramnavine hotspots, or howffs, besides public halls, where you could prop up bars, or fall slowly and with dignity down them: the Smugglers' Arms in Viggabury, and the NATO police enclave in the old, Cold War early warning station atop Vronnafirth Hill. Where you could simply be rolled down the slope to your waiting charabanc, were you incapable of walking. For four years, unless there was something on at one of the community halls, if you wished to receive bartending services you had to go to Hee Haw (obscure local slang for the urban sprawl of Brae, 10 miles to the south, feeder settlement for the giant oil terminal of Sullom Voe). We were publess, and our culture and community was seriously denuded as a result. For everywhere needs a place you can gather of an evening, casually to converse, canoodle or fight. Everywhere needs somewhere. A place where, if everybody doesn't know your name, they can, in a befuddled fashion, roughly recall your face. Cheers!

After all, in the real world, Walford has the Queen Vic, Weatherfield the Rover's Return and Cicely Alaska had The Brick. Strange things happen, or happened in all three establishments, but only in the Brick were you likely to find yourself rubbing shoulders with ghosts and medicine men, pathological liars who were also internationally acclaimed uberchefs, female floatplane pilots who looked like the young Brigitte Bardot, ex-astronauts with Mars-sized chips on their shoulders, former golf pros, a native Indian film buff with a Woody Allen complex, and of course a displaced New York doctor whose neuroses made Woody Allen's appear laughably minor league. Oh, and there were bears, flying men, and especially an ex-jailbird philosopher called Chris who broadcast everything from Jung and Proust to Nietzsche on the local radio station, K-BHR.

For those not already going "aaahhh" and relaxing into the tragedy-free, disturbingly relaxing world of Cicely, I must tell you that the place did not really exist. The TV series *Northern Exposure* did, though, for six series in the 90s, and it was set there. All the programmes can be streamed, no doubt, but as it happens I have the complete box set on that elderly medium, DVD, and you can buy it if you like, from The Last Bookshop and DVD Emporium. It will be very expensive, though, because I don't really want to sell it, and the truth is that I wallow, periodically, in Alaskan quirkiness. I feel at home there.

All kinds of people pop up in Cicely. Sigmund Freud and the Prophet Elijah to name but two. There are long, entertaining but often rambling discussions about shamanism, dream theory, obscure eastern philosophies and the work of Ayn Rand or Jack London. Oh, and golf. There's a lot of golf. All of which should, when I first started watching the show (and Rob Morrow was Joel Fleischman, not that wee, worn fat guy in the movie *Quiz Show*) have clued me in on *Northern Exposure*'s spiritual hinterland: Joshua Brand and John Halsey, who came up with the whole concept, were members of the Esalen Institute, a kind of residential, post-hippy commune-laboratory in Big Sur, California, founded for spiritual, philosophical and psychological experimentation. And golf.

Michael Murphy, its director, wrote the classic book of 'the spiritual game', *Golf in the Kingdom*. And he understands that golf is life. Or life is golf, I forget which.

In truth, Quidawick, indeed much of rural Shetland (the capital Lerwick, to be controversial, is wondrous in many ways but does not contain the soul of Shetland; it remains, as an acquaintance put it, "a small northern Scottish town with a chip on its three shoulders") bears many comparisons with the bewitching world of *Northern Exposure*. True, the ghosts of Elijah and Freud do not regularly make appearances here, but like that mythical vision of Alaska, this is where all kinds of folk are blown in by literal and metaphorical hurricanes, and never leave. Bringing with them their words, their music, their pictures, their foibles and fantasies, their brilliance and stupidity, their crackpot theories and blinding insights. All of which can be merged, melded or just mixed up with the native products, sometimes to inspiring effect. And sometimes it all ends in flouncings-out, fisticuffs, divorce and embarrassing drunken scenes in bars.

There was a second bar in Quidawick, many years ago, called Da Ben End. A gloriously traditional, peat-fire-warmed repository of 'characters', with the occasional live band and a strict rule banning you from breaking the free crab claw snacks on the polished wood counter. It is long shut and one of those mythical, lost drinking establishments. You pass the former premises now and there's not even the hint of what used to go on there – the swinging pool cues, crunching rock music and sweet traditional fiddle playing, pyramids of used McEwen's Export tins and the invention of the legendary Bailey's Challenge, where the aim was to down an entire bottle of Bailey's Cream Liqueur, run outside, then vomit it all up in a constant stream while spinning around, executing a perfect circle of recycled alcoholic dairy product. Fortunately, this fine tradition is still pursued just down the road in Hee Haw. But we invented it in Quidawick. Oh yes.

But as I gazed through into the darkened, abandoned Ronnie's, I was still able to see the ghosts of drinkers and landlords past. The owner (one of many) who sold it with a 'full stocked bar' which was discovered to mean that every spirit bottle remaining on the gantry had been filled with liquid of indeterminate origin and unknown toxicity. The famous packet soup served in the restaurant by one chef who would cheerfully claim that it had been 'customised'. That time a 'birthday bus' arrived with its addled contents, all young men from the island of Garbisay celebrating someone's 18th, and pelted two unsuspecting tourists with the contents of dogmeat cans, screaming "welcome to Shetland" at them. The bonfire night celebration where inebriated setting-off-of-fireworks sent a toppled coastguard flare through the bar entrance, where it exploded in a massive red eruption and was completely ignored by the two catatonic drinkers remaining on their stools. That time the police were called when two 85-year-old men attacked each other with darts. And so on.

Inevitably, the St Rognvald had to be reopened, reborn. I made an offer for the place myself. £14,000. The owner, some mysterious inhabitant of Leicester, laughed down the line and then slammed the phone down. For a long time I favoured the notion of being a curmudgeonly landlord, with some redeeming features (free drinks on Christmas Eve? The occasional buckshee packet of past-sell-by-date crisps?). Some of us fantasised about seeking Highlands and Islands Enterprise funding so a deputation could fly to Alaska in an attempt to find Cicely (though the truth is *Northern Exposure* was shot in and based on the community of Roslyn, Washington State) and investigate the possibility of replicating that seminal TV programme's pub-café The Brick in Ramnavine. I could re-invent myself as Holling Vincoeur.

And then Alicia and Pedro came along. And the St Rognvald did not, after all, become something from a TV series. Nowadays it's much, much better than that.

Ronnie's is now a renowned Sunday lunch destination year-round for Shetlanders, with its legendary carvery (unlimited second helpings, and only £15 per person) and a guaranteed friendly welcome from Alicia, native Shetlander and mistress of real, non-packet soup, and her husband Pedro, a former marine engineer whose taste in malt whisky now adds a real lustre to the gantry which once boasted nothing but Generic Alcoholic Stuff.

The old wooden building, its honeyed pine internal panelling aglow in the light of glamorous chandeliers, is always busy, with many of its residents long-stay workers engaged in construction work at the Sullom Voe oil terminal. But it's a favourite with tourists, too, and winter and summer offers comfortable accommodation, a well-stocked bar and excellent, exceedingly generous helpings of food. But when Alicia and Pedro took over the St Rognvald in 2007, things were very different. Empty for four years, the unique all-pine structure was rotting away. There were gaps in the walls and leaks in the roof. It was cold, all year round.

"It was a nasty, freezing autumn day when we first got inside," says Alicia. "The hotel had been very badly neglected by the owners before us, and then lay empty for four years. We just looked around and said: 'What have we done?'"

I am convinced that, as soon as this delightful spot becomes known, it will be a favourite resort for tourists in search of fine air, quiet and comfort.

The story told about the St Rognvald has always been this: it was a flat-pack, sectional building, floated up on a barge from Glasgow, where it had been dismantled after serving as the Norwegian Pavilion at the 1896 Great Exhibition. It was supposed to have a twin, perched on the edge of a Scandinavian fjord, destroyed in a fire. But it's a tale which Alicia and Pedro, having spent eight years tearing the old building apart and putting it back together again, have come to doubt.

"That's the folklore," says Alicia, "but as we've been carrying out the renovations that's not what the evidence suggests. If that was true you'd expect it to be bolted together but in fact it's all nailed, and there's no scarring of the wood where previous nails have been drawn, so either they put it together second time around with bigger nails in exactly the same places, or maybe it's just folklore, and it was maybe another hotel floated north. Maybe the St Rognvald came here in that form on a barge but we suspect it has always been more Scottish than Norwegian, though it's built in a Norwegian style."

It's true that in late Victorian times there was a trend for 'instant' hunting and fishing hotels to be erected in Scotland using wooden frames and cladding – notably the Barony Hotel on Birsay and another Orcadian establishment which once bore an amazing resemblance to the St Rognvald, and was also owned by the North of Scotland, Orkney and Shetland Steam Navigation Company, known as 'The North Company' or 'The North of Scotland'.

"We think the Standing Stones Hotel in Orkney was the one which used parts of the Norwegian pavilion from 1896," says Pedro. "The stories about that building's origin are the same as this one, but it's two or three years older than ours, and it can only really be true of one hotel. In old photographs, the similarity with the St Rognvald is incredible. We know this building was put up by contractors from Shetland and in charge was the celebrated Shetlander Gideon J Halfpenny-Goodlad, who designed many major Lerwick buildings – like the Central Hotel, the Deanston School and most of King Jotun Street. He was also heavily involved in constructing the lesser-known lighthouses and other major buildings."

Indeed Gideon J Halfpenny-Goodlad was one of the most important Shetlanders of his time. He was born and died in Lerwick, but trained as an architect in Edinburgh and his firm handled everything in island construction. One early advert described him as 'architect, surveyor, appraiser, builder, joiner, funeral director, preacher, water diviner and plumber.'

The new hotel has a distinctly picturesque appearance, being built... entirely of wood. The nut-brown colour of the outer walls is grateful to the eye, and the yellow brick chimneys and gray-blue slates of the roof afford a pleasant contrast.

Alicia agrees that essentially the St Rognvald is an Halfpenny-Goodlad design. "It opened in July 1900 and we have a copy of the first page of the register. And his name is there, plainly stated – it says 'GJ Halfpenny-Goodlad, architect of this hotel'. Also, we've had many Norwegian people visiting who have told us that if it was truly Norwegian it would be finished in far fancier panelling – the panelling used is fairly plain Scots pine v-lining."

But never mind the facts, what about the legend? Is it possible that the tale of the floating flat-pack Norwegian hotel could, just, maybe, be true?

Alicia laughs. "It's possible it could have been, but we doubt it because we have ripped this place apart in a way nobody else has to try and keep it alive for another hundred years, and we were always looking for the physical evidence. We never found it. An awful lot of the original timbers have been rotted beyond saving and have had to be replaced, though you can't tell by looking at it."

So why was this 33-bedroom hotel built in Quidawick, at a time when the road from Lerwick had not been completed and indeed, the nearest port of call by the 'North of Scotland' was Viggabury (steamers later came into Redskerry and delivered passengers to the hotel's own extendable pier by flit-boat)? Well, the steamship company wanted to extend its operations into the fashionable hunting, shooting and fishing market, and as in Orkney, advertised the St Rognvald as a 'resort and spa'.

"They advertised hunting, shooting, fishing, walking and general outdoor leisure pursuits," says Alicia. "There used to be a croquet lawn – we found the original croquet set during the renovations. There was a golf course where the health centre is and then over onto the Quidawick Ness. They had a launch on Hjalda Voe, boats for sea fishing, and boats on the hill lochs with local folk employed as ghillies. The guests were wealthy folk. Normal people didn't have holidays back in those days – they'd be lucky to get a day off so it was all people with serious money. The gentry."

The North of Scotland company was taken over by P&O, who sold off the hotel in the early 1970s to the first of four private owners who have had custody of the building. "I think that improved the hotel," says Pedro, "as it was operated year round instead of just the summer. It was originally only open from May until early September, and lying empty during the cold winters must have done damage. There was no insulation or central heating in those days. Former owners have told us that when they were running it in the winter it pretty much bankrupted them, trying to keep open and warm – whatever they made went up the chimneys in fuel and burning coal."

Alicia: "The folk we took over from were running a coach company in England and they did the least to the building of all the private owners. It really had been sadly neglected latterly, though the first two owners after the North of Scotland did a lot. But we got it after a decade without any but the most basic maintenance so, first and foremost, we had to make it wind and watertight. Things were so bad we had to prioritise. It's been a long uphill slog, but we're getting there now, I think."

The interior of the hotel... is luxurious in the best sense of the word. The appointments are handsome without being pretentious, and very good taste has been shown in the selection of the furniture, carpets etc. everything looking, as it is, thoroughly good.

"We can never stop, though," says Pedro. "It's in the nature of hotels – they need to be constantly renewing themselves. It's not uncommon for a hotel to close down for two or three years for a complete refit after 25 years in operation. Unfortunately, we're very involved in the oil industry and they need the rooms – all the hotels in Shetland have the same problem. They have to keep open and keep working and the buildings just get worn out. We have hundreds or even thousands of people a week trudging through the hotel and we have no choice – we have to keep working. But we have the added problem that it's a wooden building, so we have to pay a little bit more care and attention and spend more money than maybe a block or stone built building would need.

"We're getting there. The main engineering has all been renewed – all the plumbing, heating, electrical, systems, fire alarms, sprinklers – everything has been replaced and is brand new, and performing really well. We have emergency generators. We keep

126

our own underground supply of fuel to get through the winters. Being in Shetland you never know what the winters will bring."

The recent oil and gas boom in Shetland, centred on the Sullom Voe Terminal and the Laggan-Tormore gas project, has brought a huge amount of business to the hotel. What does the future hold?

Pedro thinks that despite the downturn in oil prices there will still be hydrocarbon-related business for the St Rognvald. "To me, the future of the oil industry seems if anything more secure today in Shetland. When we bought the hotel we had no idea Total was about to turn up on the island and start work on the gas processing plant. Now, in the seas around Shetland there are multiple new oil finds that are apparently going to take the industry onwards for next 10 years or so. Whether the oil industry will continue to use small hotels like ours is another question. But our ultimate plan is to get the hotel back to the quality it would have been when originally built and perhaps even improve it. I mean, we can make the building warm now, all year round. And in 1900 there was no wifi or television."

So perhaps Quidawick will once again become an attraction for the wealthy of the world. Pedro and Alicia have even looked into providing a daily seaplane service from Glasgow direct to the St Rognvald. Of course, the hotel not only employs many local people, but serves them too, and not just with food and drink.

Pedro's proud of the St Rognvald's self-reliance and commitment to the community. "We've built the hotel to be almost self-contained. It's always able to function in bad weather – if there's a power failure, or the internet is down, whatever, we find local folk coming in and using facilities because they know they are always working – we always have power and gas," (a bottled gas supply company is run from the building) "and we have broadband because we have satellite, so it works if the BT connection has been damaged by trawlers or whatever."

Just one last question: the St Rognvald was always known as the 'White Hotel', and the renewal of the outer wooden panelling has seen it left unpainted. Why?

For Alicia, it's all about being faithful to the history of the building. "It wasn't white originally. In fact, it's been all kind of terrible colours. It's been lemon and it's been green, but originally it is described as a 'nut brown building, glistening in the sunshine' – and we've seen pieces of the original, unpainted timber. So the colour it is now is the way it was in 1900."

All I can tell you is this: the St Rognvald is not just my local, it is a source of customers here at The Last Bookshop, a place of sustenance and succour, especially on Sundays when Alicia's legendary carvery is available. It has an excellent selection of malt whiskies, St Mungo's Glasgow lager on tap, and when the power goes off and the wifi is down, their generator works and their satellite wifi functions. It has the best chips in the UK, unless you're some kind of taste-averse mutant who likes those horrible frozen things best.

Of course, it's not really called the St Rognvald. Otherwise I'd just be advertising. Otherwise too many people might come and disturb my greatest pleasure, which is sitting in the old bar in a gale, hearing the old place creak and very nearly sway, sipping a Highland Park, and wondering about ghosts. And chips.

All quotes in italics from an article in the Aberdeen Free Press, Sept 5, 1900

Engineer

Just along from Last Books is The Last Engineer. Ernest, who as well as being an engineer (civil, retired) is a toolmaker, boatbuilder, former arms merchant, watercolourist, mountaineer, past champion road-racing cyclist

and pioneer digital photographer. His skills are amazing, legion, beyond belief.

Actually, Ernest was only ever an armourer and gun dealer for the local farming and crofting community, giving it up after a young man tried to convince him he needed an elephant gun "for the rabbits". Now his weaponry is only for personal use. Though come to think of it, I was told that Ernest did once make a functioning cannon. I don't think he sold it to any trigger-or-cannonball-happy terrorists. He periodically takes his English Civil War musket up Vronnafirth Hill and fires it, the resultant explosion so loud you'd think God was calling things to order. Sternly. Seals pop up, inquisitively (which is why they were so easy to shoot, back when you could shoot them. Well, actually, if you're a salmon farmer, you still can, sometimes). Birds shriek into the sky. Books fall off shelves here at The Last Bookshop. I don't suffer a heart attack. Not yet.

Ernest took me bouldering a few years ago. He's a man in his 70s, stocky and very, very strong. He is prodigiously skilled, capable, as my friend Dean, says "of doing anything he sets his mind to." And he has done almost everything, including some activities which to most folk would seem obscure, but to Ernest are just part of life's everyday fabric. One day I mentioned that there had been less local gunfire than usual, coming from his direction.

"Ah," he replied, "that's because I've gone back to the archery."

Archery, Ernest? I had no idea.

"Well, the Ribble Valley was the home of the English longbow. Men from our village were legally obliged to keep up their skills, and you can still see the banks of earth where the targets were. When I were a lad we used to calculate the parabolic arc needed for your Battle of Hastings type longbow attack. It's in the blood."

Another time, I was round at the smithy and Ernest happily demonstrated his latest acquisition, the hooter from an old Inter City diesel train, one of the legendary Deltics. I was so astonished by its existence I forgot to ask where he'd got it. Possibly eBay, or perhaps it floated ashore at the back of Quidawick Ness on an inflated dinosaur stomach. Anyway, all across our little seaside crafting community came the ferociously loud whoop of a massive passenger train. The sheep were startled, to say the least.

I'm aware this sounds kind of unlikely, but people acquire strange things around here. Or strange things arrive here by uncertain means. A crofter friend was checking the rear of his sileage container the other day when he found a lifejacket, the kind you get on aeroplanes, clearly marked 'Lufthansa'. It was dirty and old, and how it came to be there remains a complete mystery.

How our friend Rankin obtained the 50-seater piston engined airliner that sits proudly in front of his house in Redskerry, and is used as a very particular kind of shed, is no mystery at all. Abandoned for years at Sumburgh Airport, latterly used for fire training, he asked if he could have it, hired a low-loader, and shipped it the 80 miles or so north to his front garden. How he explained the whole thing to his wife I do not know. But he'd always been interested in aircraft.

Ernest had offered to take me bouldering, as I'd casually mentioned that I'd never done any rock climbing and always had a vague desire to try it, without actually using ropes (too complicated) or killing myself (too sore).

And so it was that one bright June morning, Ernest turned up at the door. "Right? Fine dry day. The rock should be sound."

Being hungover after a night demonstrating the wonders of The Masters Wine Club to local hotelier Francisco (supplier of much vinyl for The Record Shop at The Edge of The World), I was in no mood for it. But Ernest has a habit of being impossible to refuse. So I dragged my unwilling, frazzled bulk out to his van, and we set off.

"Me and Egbert, back in the 70s, there's not a face in the North Mainland we didn't climb," mused Ernest, driving his ancient van at dangerously high speeds down the single track road that leads south of Baywick, a series of clangs and thumps from the back indicating the presence of who knew what kind of equipment – possibly more bits of diesel train, ancient steam hammers or medieval pikes. "Covered in fulmar spew we'd get, like bloody spiders we were... terrible risk, mind, some of that rock is treacherous. But Egbert, before he went south, he was some boy for leading, right up to VS – Very Severe."

"Where did you learn to climb, Ernest?"

"Ah well," his foot eased slightly on the accelerator. "Yorkshire dales and crags, and of course, there was the caving. Did that first, member of cave rescue, and some of the lads got me into climbing. One thing leads to the other."

Caving, archery, cycle racing, motorbike racing, boat manufacture (and I've seen Ernest's hand-built, ocean-going wooden fishing boats; they're magnificent, and both sold to southern collectors), not to mention the manufacture – by hand forging – of a full-size traditional naval anchor one year and 12 months later, an anvil. And of course there were the traction engines.

One thing truly does lead to another.

Soon we were engaged in what I remember doing as a child: pretending to rock climb, basically, a few feet and sometimes inches off the ground, clambering around low faces among about 20 dead sheep ("crofters... don't bloody feed them in the winter and that's what happens... either that or struck by lightning... my money's on the crofters"). Soon, fingers are sore and grazed, but it's fun. Then, like the child I once was, I soon get

bored. If we're going to go rock climbing, we need the risk, I say. Though I'm a bit concerned about the vertigo I sometimes suffer from. The perpetual presence of death is bound to add a tad more interest than not falling a

foot or so into the soft Shetland bogland.

"Aye," says Ernest. "Remember, though. It's not the height that kills you. It's the depth."

A statement I have pondered, earnestly, ever since.

"I remember once in the lakes," Ernest says, as we sit on a relatively dry patch of springy heather, "...watched one of those army young leader groups tackling a face, I think it was in Borrowdale somewhere. Bad rock, black and wet. Difficult. Just dried out enough for us to get up, no problems, and we were back at the bottom ready for the off, like, when one of their lads got into trouble. Got stuck. We could hear the shouting, commotion, like. And we would have helped, maybe gone back up, but it had started to rain again. But we watched. And one of our lads, he had a pair of bins, Leitz – always liked the best that lad, farrier from Leeds – focussed on the stuck lad, and he says, 'Christ Ernest, take a look at that.' And passes them over.

"So I have a look, and this lad, stuck he is, but somehow he's got the rope round his neck, and he's twitching there, legs all over the place, hands under the rope, trying to relieve the pressure. Face going black. Bloody hell. Anyway, mountain rescue arrives, but he's dead. Strangled. Hanged himself. Bloody fuss over that, I can tell you."

I'm thinking of the stories I've heard about the Clydeside mountaineers, the iron-forged workers from shipyards and foundries who, after World War Two, discovered the transcendent glories and physical demands of the mountains on their doorstep. These were hard, hard men, and often they had the most basic of equipment or none at all. Life was cheap, both in the yards and on the hills; if anyone slipped and fell, on some of the most popular faces, like Ardvorlich or The Cobbler, there was – or so the stories go – sometimes a scramble to strip the still-warm corpse of rope, boots or anything else usable.

There's a tale of one man falling a considerable way, to attract immediate attention from would-be salvagers, only for a weak voice to tell them: "Leave us alane, ye bastards. Ah'm no deid yet."

Here in The Last Bookshop, The Emporium at The Edge of The World, I'm wondering if I'll go bouldering again. Ernest, on that last expedition, voiced the suspicion that, given various back problems, he might not be able to manage it himself that often. And something I've realised about Ernest is this: he tells the truth. It's one of the things people find annoying about him. He is the real deal. He really has done all this stuff, he really can do it. And if he says he may not be able to he means that too.

But he can still take photographs, one of his more recent passions. And the ones I have on the wall of The Bookshop are quite extraordinary.

There's the Hoor's Ratchet, a rocky islet off Karaness which, from most shoreside angles, looks like a whale, but from one view has a giant arch cut through it. It's maybe 200 metres long, and Ernest has a picture – I have a picture – of waves breaking over it. I won't translate the name. You can guess.

That doesn't come close to doing the image justice. It was taken during a hurricane, and Ernest had his camera wrapped in clingfilm as he waited hours for just the right moment. The result shows the Ratchet dwarfed by waves that look as though they could sink a supertanker. And maybe they did.

The weird thing is, though, that unless you know the Hoor's Ratchet, the picture is not as impressive as it might be. It's not as if the waves are breaking over the Houses of Parliament, though that's the scale of motion we're talking about. It's a picture which draws gasps of amazement from Ramnavine locals, but visitors tend to pass by without comment. Until they've been to Karaness themselves.

Ernest's close-ups of otters are lovely, his big sellers. But I love the picture of a waterspout shooting maybe 60 feet in the air from the ground in front of the Karaness lighthouse. Ernest waited a whole day for this, the highly unusual action of a blowhole in the clifftop, a tunnel running from a cave below through to the cliff hundreds of feet above. As far as I know, it's the only time anyone has ever photographed the phenomenon.

And yet, again, it's one of those pictures which has to be explained. That locals love it as a souvenir of the extreme, sometimes bizarre natural conditions they live in the midst of. But to any casual viewer it

looks slightly faked.

Like Ernest, though, it's real; the genuine, untouched article.

Investors

It's important, for the future of Shetland, to attract newcomers to the islands, people who, like me, will settle here and become part of the community. Hopefully strengthening it and providing money and resources for longer-term residents and natives to appropriate. It is one of the functions, I hope, of this book, to make the islands seem attractive, or at least to make you curious enough to visit, come to The Last Bookshop and give us – me – some of your hard-earned money. In fact, it doesn't have to be hard-earned. Easy come, easy go is fine by me.

If you've reached this far in *In Shetland*, you'll have gained a flavour of the place, I hope. I haven't mentioned too many of Shetland's great inventions such as the fish-gutting machine which was the product of a brilliant man called Jim Smith, or Jim O'Berry. He was one of those self-educated geniuses that pop up in remote spots. He designed and built not one but two of his own aeroplanes, from scratch. One of them even flew.

And smallpox inoculation began here, courtesy of the character known as Johnnie Notions. Erving Goffman invented modern micro-sociology after a summer spent working on the island of Yell. And of course, the internet was invented in Scalloway (along with, allegedly, the concept of the Scalliwag; but that's another story). To be precise, it is alleged that power circuit networking was invented by an engineer there – that's the business of using home electrical circuits to send your broadband from room to room. I've been told that this was an accidental discovery made when one BT engineer wired a telephone into the mains by mistake. But when I put this to BT management they said such an allegation was "shocking".

Anyway, to provide a break from all this prose, I thought I might introduce one or two poems, thus providing an askew view on some aspects of Shetland life. And to start off, I thought I'd tackle the question of the Shetland beard. The beard is, of course, a highly desirable, if not essential component of the Up Helly Aa festivities, though it can pose certain risks. Who can forget the great Guizer Jarl chin conflagration of 1958, and the consequent banning of Vaseline to provide added shine to one's manly growth?

Welcome to Shetland, land of the beard
Where weak jawlines are made to disappear
And chins, quadruple down to double
Sprout wispy, weedy down, or fearsome stubble
The kind that leaves a rash or even scars
The casual kisser, or removes the paint from cars
Should face and body work collide
Some small refreshment having been imbibed

It can take many months, or even years
To grow a quite convincing Viking beard
And would be Norsemen, filled with fear and doubt
Their naked chins refusing to sprout
Resort to desperate measures, pills and ointments
To counter any hairless disappointment
Hormone supplements, consumed in quantities
So vast, they've opened special pharmacies

Male pattern baldness, fought by men down south
Means nothing here, it's whiskers round the mouth
Which mark the man of honour, poise and strength
No wonder here we'll go to any length
Those bristles to obtain
Suffer any pain
Abrasion with sandpaper will
Used with a Black and Decker drill

Stimulate, I'm told those Viking follicles
It's a fact, historical, absolute and true
It worked for me. I pray it works for you

Shetland's transportation network is for the most part excellent, and includes inter island ferries, a small and noisy aeroplane to connect the outer isles with Chinese takeaway providers, and of course the stretches of tarmac often referred to as 'roads'. This is where a great deal of the Council's income from decades of putting up with the oil industry has gone. There are two potholes in Shetland, one in the Co-op car park in Brae, one in the Co-op car park in Lerwick. That one actually takes up most of the Co-op Car Park in Lerwick. But there is the question of the ultimate Shetlandic vehicle. What is it? It can only be one thing…

Once this addiction starts
I cannot stop
I need an Ifor Williams top
Though never will a sheep or dog,
Woman or child
Scratch my tailgate

I hate the thought
Of grubby paws, or bags of Tesco shopping
Scarring the luscious Mitsubishi sheen.
I've been there. I had a HiLux once,
A crew cab, with roll-bar, shotgun rack
Springsteen, Steve Earle and Daniel O'Donnel tracks
Red tins of beer

It ended in tears:
A wife, a collie, trips sooth to IKEA
Talk of baby seats and daft ideas
Concerning Citröens, Peugeots, or worse
A Vauxhall Zafira
I did not hear her

For I was gone, long gone
Working offshore in Venezuela
My relationship a failure

But I saved sufficient cash
For a Barbarian, with leather seats
The sound so sweet
Of its diesel engine in my ears
Crankshaft and gasket failure fears
Assuaged (That was in the early L200 years)

And so I drive from North Roe down to Sumburgh
And back, in only clement weather
I'll wash her with the finest chamois leather
And in the heated garage
Stroke her gently

She's better than a Bentley
Or Nissan, or Toyota
Not one iota of regret
Do I feel
This love is real
I count my blessings and my luck
In finding you, my one true pick-up truck
My L200
My precious! Do not fear
I'll never over-rev you in third gear

(And, when launching a boat into the sea,
I promise not to reverse you down
Door-deep, until your footwells are awash
With salty water
Which, long ago, I did.
Warned many times, I just refused to listen
However, that truck was leased, and besides
It was a Nissan)

During the first referendum campaign (2014, the one about whether or not Alex Salmond should ever be allowed to wear a kilt again, or just trews), which you may remember, a journalist came to see me. Indeed, I used to work for him, when I too was a journalist, before I became a light entertainer. He had come to Shetland as part of a state of the nation tour of Scotland, and I was happy to make him some lunch, introduce him to the St Bernards, give him a cloth to wipe the drool off his Paul Smith suit and Rohan anorak. He wrote a fairly innocuous piece at the time, and it wasn't until a few months later, in a column, that he revealed how much he hated Shetland, hated me, hadn't enjoyed his lunch and was forced to throw away his trousers due to the acidic qualities of St Bernard slobber. But there was another reason, I felt, why he didn't like Shetland. He got a knockback in Posers.

Or rather, from Posers. Posers is a nightclub. Posers is THE Shetland nightclub. And what a name it is! Worthy of Ibiza. Or Orkney. When I first came to the isles, almost 30 years ago, I was used to Glasgow nightclubs and when I heard we were going to one in Shetland I dressed accordingly – Levis 501s, polished Docs, Cruise leather jacket. Got to the door, and the bouncer said, "Sorry sir, you can't come in wearing that. Or those." I was forced to remove my jacket and my shoes, and put on a pair of strange funeral brogues. Walked in and the first thing I saw was two guys at the bar, wearing boiler suits and wellington boots.

Edinburgh man hates Shetland
Too much building work
Cranes and bulldozers
Besides, they wouldn't let him into Posers
Not dressed like that
In Boden and Hackett
You'll have to remove that jacket, sir
And all your clothes
It speaks of values we don't share
Look, we have Fair Isle you can wear
Admittedly a little itchy

As underwear
But it's compulsory soothmoothers must learn
To love the constant rubbing, the knitwear burn
On naked skin
You'll soon fit in
Scar tissue forms quite quickly
True, you may feel sickly for a while
But smile. And have a dance
It's a Boston two step!
Now's your chance!
You see, how stimulating
Wool on bare skin can be?
You'll recover soon
It's just minor surgery

Just one final verse before I (for a brief spell) return to joined-up writing, and this one concerns my own assimilation into the ways of Shetland fashion. The padded lumberjack shirt. The Dickies jeans. The unavailable-anywhere-else Wolsey bri-nylon underwear. Oh, the freedom! The static electricity! The rash…

What a relief
When I came to this place
To wear comfortable trousers
With elasticated waists
No need for ties
Or Armani suits
You could go the Jubilee
Wearing Wellington boots
Preferably white
With optional fish scales
Or Yellow, but not black or green
Those would fail
Any bouncer's test
And for boiler suits
Blue was the best

Under the black light
It looked kind of cool
But no leather jackets
That was the rule
Because leather was evil
Leather was bad
It made people violent
It made people mad
Back in the days before
Jaegermeister, Magners or Aftershock
It was leather made young people
Knock off each other's blocks

Now we slump on sofas
In pullups and baffies
Lerwick still has one nightclub
And 17 cafés
Commercial Street runs with
Lattes and cappuccinos
Councillors are wearing
Hugo Boss and Moschino
Still, I wear North Eastern Farmers
And LHD proudly
And play Daniel O'Donnell records
At home now
Quite loudly

Geese

Fergus, a visiting recycler of chipfat, said he would kill the goose, as he had experience.

"Experience of what?"

"Killing things" he said.

"What things?"

He pondered for a moment. "Mostly annoying insects. But at least that shows I'm prepared to extinguish life. I'm not a Buddhist. We have a midge-eating machine at home. Millions of the beasties can die in a week. I'm a mass murderer, and what's more, I've never felt a twinge of guilt."

I looked at him. I thought of my own bloodstained recent past. Helping out local crofters I had wielded shotgun and knife. Either personally or standing by while the act was committed. Pigs. Sheep. Black-back gulls. Ducks. Cows. Dogs. Cats. Many fish.

"I'll do it," I said.

Fergus looked momentarily disconsolate. "I've always wanted to kill a mammal," he said. "It's part of one's development as a human being. As a man. It's a ritual, isn't it? Iron John, dancing naked in firelight, smeared in blood, out of our heads on magic mushrooms and whisky. Like a Jackie Leven song. Hemingway. That hippy guy out of Take That, the one that went whale spotting."

"It's that Charles Manson thing you're really looking for, isn't it?"

Fergus was a city boy, 10 years younger than me, and an acquaintance of an acquaintance, a fairly normal person called Ian, who was a drug dealer in Glasgow. Folk like Fergus tend to turn up on your doorstep in places like Shetland, convinced you'll be delighted to see an emissary from civilisation, or Glasgow. He'd claimed to be in the islands at the invitation of Highlands and Islands Enterprise, HIE, to look at a proposed project that would see half of Shetland's farm vehicles running on bio-diesel made from old cooking oil. For this he claimed to be receiving £300 a day plus expenses.

Neither he nor HIE appeared to know that, in sheds throughout the islands, crofters were using white spirit and stoves to turn every millilitre of fish-smelling chip shop and cafe fat residue they could beg or steal into something that would run a Citroen Berlingo HDI. He was a consultant, after all. Let him consult. Wasn't it a kind of metaphysical crofting?

"Charles Manson, yes!" said Fergus, eagerly. "Is he from here?"

"Fergus, tell me you know who Charles Manson is?"

A pause. Then, "Manson. Is that a Shetland name?"

"Leader of a druggy black magic cult in California in the 60s. The Family. The Sharon Tate murders? You must have heard of them? Roman Polanski's wife? Eight and a half months pregnant?"

Fergus nodded. "Err... no. But were geese involved?"

"Not that I know of."

"Can I at least have a go of your shotgun?"

"It's not mine. I've just borrowed it. In case any drug dealers turn up here, unexpectedly."

"Oh."

I began to feel slightly perturbed. Consultants will do that to you. In Shetland, hospitality to strangers, even to the evidently infirm, even to visiting chipfat boilers on £300 a day, is compulsory. But it has its limits. Fergus had arrived that Saturday morning in a hired Kia, checked out of his hotel, the weekend stretching before him until his flight home on Monday morning. I had given him coffee, some soda bread, talked about our mutual semi-friends, and then stupidly mentioned that this was the day of reckoning for our geese, Gordon and Tony.

"Fergus? Can I ask you a question?"

"Yes?"

"Have I told you our rates? Did Ian (drug dealer) mention that at all?"

"Rates? Rates for what?"

"Well, for the whole crofting experience package. That's what you're here for, isn't it? Ian recommends people every year. No charge for the coffee, of course, but the soda bread's homemade and that's a fiver. Accommodation in the barn – fresh hay and heather, you'll sleep like a baby – is £75, the full goose killing, plucking and preparation, with dinner, is another 40 quid. Bring your own bottle. Or you can have some of our homemade wine, I've forgotten how much Susan charges for that."

There was a silence. Fergus looked slightly pained, as if he was trying to work something out. I guessed it was to do with his daily expenses claim from HIE, and whether hay or heather in the barn (in November) would compare well with the Busta House Hotel's duvets.

"Do you know," he said, "do you know, I think I'll maybe head back down to Brae. There's a chip shop there may be interested in hearing about the possibilities of profitably utilising their waste."

I didn't think so. All the oil from Frankie's went to powering an old Land Rover and a Mercedes taxi. But I'd let him fail to find that out for himself. Because nobody would be telling him anything. That's what makes consultants so entertaining, if not very useful.

I waved him off towards Brae and the – artificial fibre, not goose down – duvets of Busta House. I was a fiver up on his visit. I'd need to tell Ian, the next time we met, not to hand out my whereabouts to every Fergus, Kieran and Jocasta he came across. Still, a fiver a visit was almost worth it. That soda bread was damn good, though. And, you know… 'the full crofting experience package' had a nice ring to it. Maybe I could get some kind of grant to find out whether such a thing was a touristic possibility. Meanwhile, it was a good day for Tony and Gordon to die. I went to the back cupboard where I'd stored (illegally) my neighbour Methven's shotgun.

Geese are horrid things. Everyone says they're useful and beautiful, and that they're the best watchdogs you can get. That aren't dogs. They are aggressive, and bulky. In fact, for years I thought that a flap of their wing could break a child's leg, because my mother, who was half-Irish, would insist that this was the case. In fact, though, she was referring to a swan, which can and does break human limbs of all kinds up to and including an adult leg. If that adult has osteoporosis. One flap and it's crunch, you're Douglas Bader. You shouldn't mess around with swans. And you mustn't eat them either, even if one flies into an electricity cable and drops dead at your feet, presumably smashing your toes to smithereens. Swans are royal birds, and only the Queen (and presumably her household) is permitted to swallow a swan nugget. Though the composer Sir Roger Maxwell Davies, who lives off and on (mostly off) the Orkney island of Hoy, once did find a newly dead whooper swan and roasted it for a quick snack. He wasn't charged with stealing from the royal salivation, or anything. Just forced to listen to nothing but Radiohead albums for a week.

There used to be a whisky warehouse on the outskirts of Glasgow that was guarded by a flock of geese, on the basis that a similar flock, some time previously, saved Rome from the Gauls. This was in 390BC, and they were being used to protect the temple of Juno from marauding neds. There's still a sacred flock of geese in Rome, in case of rampaging protestants.

Geese are everywhere in myth and fable. The goose that laid the golden egg, goosey goosey gander (wandering, ahem upstairs, downstairs and in my lady's chamber. Missus!). And of course when Aphrodite first came ashore she was welcomed by the Charities, appropriately enough, in a chariot, towed by geese.

And what, you may ask, did all these geese, sacred and profane, have in common (with the possible exception of the one that is a metaphor for the penis)? I'll tell you. They shat, defaecated, did great big jobbies, copiously, constantly and absolutely everywhere. And they ate every shred of greenery they could. Yes, they are ideal substitutes for lawnmowers, if you don't mind you r lawnmower depositing tons of excrement on every square foot of cropped grass, turning your patch of garden into a gigantic toxic waste dump, inhabited only by large, flapping, squawking creatures with wings that could break a child's... fingernail.

They are, however, easy to shoot. Unlike hens, but that's another story. So I did shoot them, using Methven's Mossberg pump action single barrel which has, by law, been restricted to three shots, instead of the five it was designed to take for the purposes of holding up convenience stores in its native Unites States of Avarice. Methven told me he bought it in very strange little second-hand gun shop in Dundee, along with a 12-bore Laurona and a Glock automatic pistol ("perfect for slaughtering cows"). Presumably that was a well, under the counter sale, though I know Methven has a certificate, which is not that easy to get hold of. However, being a crofter, and having a wee bit of land, the ability to make satisfying loud bangs and blast lumps out of coke cans after a few beers remains a privilege worth, at least for Methven, the five-yearly hassle with references, and a note from your doctor stating that you're of sound mind and are allowed only to go out shooting after the one bottle of whisky.

Anyway, Methven lends out his shotgun for a bottle of whisky, too, so that's all right.

Later on, when Susan came home from the surgery, she found me up to my proverbial oxters in goose down.

"Quick!" she said, "get a bag. Sterilise them in the microwave, and it'll be lovely to sleep on that tonight!"

I let her collect the feathers while I concentrated on preparing the deceased geese for, respectively, the freezer and the oven.

Deliciousness ensued. A chunky wee Chilean Cab Sauv to go with it, and an Aberlour a'Bunadh to finish. The only thing to mar the evening was a telephone call from Fergus.

"Hallo," he said. "I'm in Busta House. Charles here at reception here says he's never heard of your 'Full Crofting Experience Package'. Otherwise he'd have sent you some customers."

"It's new," I said. "In fact, you were our first customer."

"Oh."

"But I think it was a success."

"Well. It was very good soda bread. I was wondering, if maybe tomorrow I could come and have, say, half a day's crofting experience, and perhaps handle your shotgun? A bit? Would that be possible? My last day in Shetland?"

I heard his hopeful, heavy breathing on the line. When he called I was half way through my roast goose and red wine, and I really didn't want to prolong the conversation.

"Fergus, I'm afraid I can only offer you the Gralloching package for tomorrow."

"Really? And what does that consist of?"

"It's simply the removal of maggot-infested guts from about a dozen sheep we've been ageing for the local Norse mutton delicacy which I believe is served at Busta, called Lökken. The smell can be a tad intimidating at first, but you get used to it. We'll be doing that all day, and at the end, everyone cooks their own maggot-tenderised meat over a fire of sheep dung. It's delicious!" There was a silence. Gently, I put the phone down. Or to be precise, pressed disconnect on the digital handset.

"Lökken, eh?" said Susan. "Funny, I've never heard of that. Must be a Norwegian dish. Is it?"

"Sort of," I said. "Those Norwegians, eh? Everyone talks about how lovely those Scandinavians are, how responsible, how green and environmentally concerned. When the Norwegians just kill things. They cut down all their own forests, wiped out their inshore fisheries, fished out everyone else's herring, killed every whale in the northern and southern hemispheres, nearly, massacred the picts..."

"There's no such dish as Lökken, though, is there? And we haven't kept sheep for years."

"Possibly."

Later, in bed, I found myself overtaken by a sneezing fit. I started to sneeze, and a peculiar rash began to spread around one side of my face. I turned to my personal physician and asked for a diagnosis.

"Goose down," she said firmly. "Maybe our old sheep's wool pillows would be better, actually. There's a funny smell of gunpowder coming from these ones, anyway."

"Geese," I said. "Tasty, but more trouble than they're worth."

"Like consultants?"

"Like a consultant called Fergus, anyway. Pass me a decent pillow, please. Good night."

"Good night".

I sneezed. I didn't stop all night. It was the consultant's fault.

Escape

Sometimes you just have to get away. Just occasionally, Shetland becomes oppressive, a prison. *Escape from Devil's Island* and *Papillon* keep replaying in your head. The beauty, the loveliness, the friends, the clean air, the sheep... it's not enough. The culinary glories of the Peerie Shop Café, the Scalloway Hotel and Frankie's chipper are not enough. The curries from the Brae Takeaway and the Raba all taste the same. You find yourself ordering jalfrezis with extra chilli, then adding jalapenos when you get the food home. You dream of cities, of air that isn't moving all the time. A crowd of people where you don't recognise anyone, and no-one knows who you are.

And I'm thinking about Da Dyook, who resents going to Brae, will only go there, in fact, when he needs a new van. Which as far as I can see is once every quarter century. He repaired his Citroen 2CV van with old fishing nets, and they were more weatherproof than the rust-ridden French bodywork. It's true he married a woman from Wick, Muckle Debs, but she was a fishwife in Lerwick at the time who met him at a dance in Viggabury. She was from then on confined to Shetland, apart from hospital visits to Aberdeen, and carried out such tasks in Lerwick as Da Dyook directed her to: fetching wheelbarrows, half-ton bags of fertiliser, that sort of thing. By bus of course. But for Da Dyook, Brae was a dangerous border town, just beyond the natural causeway of the Elsi Grind, and thus not Ramnavine. It had all the danger and glamour of Kinshasa or Dodge City. There was a police station, for example. And, briefly, a mobile brothel.

The brothel proved a very temporary convenience for the huge influx of travelling workers brought in to build a new gas plant at Sullom Voe. Consisting of a large caravan, the location – next to the Gospel Hall car park – was perhaps not the wisest choice. There were complaints and the operators, a well-known provider of 'international personal comfort facilities', Madame International, was forced, to, ah withdraw.

Anyway, for Da Dyook, life south of Brae was not of much concern, except when he needed something specific, which he either sent Muckle Debs for, or ordered from Ralph the Van Man. Who was good that way. Even when asked to collect a 'parcel' from the docks, only to find it was Saddleback sow. Uncrated and not best pleased to be in Shetland.

As for me, despite the seductive charms of The Last Bookshop, I need the occasional break from island life. I need to go somewhere where distance has a meaning that doesn't involve air or sea travel. I need to smell the forests, embrace the rough bark of ancient trees. I need to get decent beer, good coffee, some urban curry and the smell of bad taxi exhaust in my lungs. And besides, I need to buy more books.

So I make trips south, once or twice a year, to book fairs and especially to Wigtown, 'Scotland's Booktown', which has one or two establishments that will do deals for wholesale operatives like myself. And with various children still in Glasgow, I will go and stay in a peculiar west end hotel called the Sandyford, drink with old pals, hang out at dubious rock'n'roll dives and fill myself up with the best curries outside Bradford and Dundee. After four days I'll get twitchy, and after six, my nerves are screaming for the sound of swooping skuas and the shuddering roar of breaking seas against immovable rock. By the time I get back on the boat north, I'm tearful with emotion, desperate to return home.

Soothlag is the desire to get to the mainland, to immerse yourself in all its luxuries and delights. Shetlag is the opposite. Smells will do it, the whiff of burning cannabis at some Edinburgh party, so redolent of peat fires. You have to try and avoid the sea, or open expanses of water. Because none of them match up, could possibly compare with the great lumpy surge of the Atlantic at

Redskerry, or the salutary sense of being exposed to the biggest, baddest ocean in the world, just ten minutes' walk from our house.

But the opposite is true too. The twitchiness that occurs on a dank winter's day, the sense of exposure on a Saturday, as you walk down Lerwick's Commercial Street recognising every single face you see. The longing to be lost.

So you leave, and you come back. Sometimes you try to leave for good, but Shetland has you by the heart. It has you by the soul. You can check out any time you like, but you can never leave, not really. And if you're tempted by the limpid light of the West Highlands, the teeming fellowship of Glasgow, the cool cultural village that is Edinburgh, you have to stop and recall those desperate nights in Inverness, struggling to erase the crash and thump of the Quidawick waves from your heart; the flicker of the Nesting Up Helly Aa torches, the smell of paraffin, the sound of fiddles flicking and humming and keening in The Lounge Bar.

My wife insists on holidays, every so often. I try to resist. I always end up in dodgy, I mean really dodgy second hand bookshops in Mallorca or Alicante. You may ask, who would want to have a bookshop in a place where it's sunny and conducive to an outdoor lifestyle? The great thing about Shetland is, the weather drives you towards bookshops. It's a good place to be outdoors, yes, but often it's better, and safer, to take shelter. And do some reading.

Anyway, if it's good weather here (an admittedly rare occurrence) I simply shut the bookshop for the hour or so it remains good. *Gone to Enjoy Weather*, I write in chalk on the blackboard I keep for this purpose. *In When In*. A brilliant, if I may so, and adaptable piece of kit, in that the rain, when it comes on, washes away the message and, within a few minutes, I will have returned anyway. After all, I can fish from the banks just along the Ness. I can walk up the hill to The Stone of Trows.

You probably think I'm making this stuff up. But I'm not. Yes, of course, I have a mobile phone, but do you think I'm giving that out to anyone, even customers? No way. I can just imagine the calls coming in, if that number ever became public: "Hallo, I'm wondering if you happen to have a copy of *The Northern*

Naturalist, by Ben Seffington, published in 1932. Also any of the early Biggles books. Or *Fly Fishing*, by JR Hartley."

Everybody needs to escape sometimes. It's what living in Shetland is for. And yes, occasionally you feel the urge to get away to a city, a landmass where you can't see or smell the ocean. But not often. And you always come back.

Home. Eventually.

I left for four years once. The day I came back, I drove off the boat, parked up and bumped into an old musical acquaintance I hadn't seen since the day I left.

"Aye aye, Tammy," he said. "Has du been awa?"

Heart

A really bad camper van. What can I tell you, I've got a thing for really bad camper vans. Or I did have, until this one. This was the last.

I've had several VW Type 2s, a memorable Renault with grass growing inside, innumerable Talbots and Fiats and Fords, breakdown-prone and always smelly inside. This was a Volkswagen, a long-wheelbase T25 someone had converted, rather neatly, from a builder's runaround. I was doing some work on the most northerly Shetland island of Unst, a house clearance, looking for books. I had driven north, found that the sale was a different day, and decided to kip in a car park next to the gloomily-named Final Checkout garage and shop. That name was an omen.

I ate a pizza and an apple pie from the local bakery, tried to sleep, and when dawn broke, decided to go for a run on my bike, which I'd brought with me. It was a cold spring morning in the northern extremities of Europe. There was a stabbing pain in my chest which I put down to a lack of protective clothing.

I got back to the van and decided to head home to Quidawick. A 15-minute drive to the ferry at Belmont, a ten minute sea crossing to the island of Yell. Seventeen miles across Yell, then 20 minutes on another ferry to get to the Shetland mainland. Half an hour and home to The Last Bookshop, feeling rather odd.

And that's when the trouble started...

I used to think
If something was heart-stoppingly exciting
That was good

Until my heart stopped
Which was admittedly exciting
But not in a good way

Actually it didn't really stop
It stuttered. Creaked, complained
Huffed, puffed
And let me down
Slowly.

I didn't fall
So much as slump. Deflated.
Crumpling, wizened
Like a cheap, end-of-party
Balloon

I am a balloon, I told myself
You are a total balloon! This is nothing
But that acid reflux you've been getting lately
Too many curries
That last vindaloo
Was nudging the chilli frontier
Burnie, burnie

But nae luck
Daughter and doctors
Insisted otherwise

So there was excitement
But it wasn't mine
It belonged, like me,
To the women of the house.
And it was soon replaced by grim efficiency
Skill and drugs

Lots of good drugs

Fast ambulances
Voices
Sharp needles
Stretchers
Electronic whines and bleeps
The shocked faces
Of neighbours
Glimpsed in passing.

Whisky's good, I mumbled
My blood
Needs thinning.
My heart needs
Unstopped.
A basic Aberlour
Even a Grouse will do

But it was like I hadn't spoken
Like ordering from a barman
Otherwise engaged
Wrestling with existentialism or East Enders,
or both.

Drugs

Not Cloppy Doggerel
Cloh-PID-o'grell
Keeps platelets from sticking
Aspirin does as well
Candy Staton, I call it
Candesartan
Maintains my heart in
Working order
On the borders of health
Betas blocked by atenolol
Stomach soothed by lanzoprazole
Which works quite well with alcohol
(Not that I drink much at all
These days)
Cholesterol races
Through my bloodstream
The fat in
There repaired
By Atorvastatin
I sleep, and no perchance
For dream I will
Nightmare on nightmare,
And no idea which pill
The cause. Still
I wallow in pharmaceuticals
And swallow

Hand

This is not pain
It's merely a reminder

A grip, tightening
A warning

Muted by nitro glycerine
Under the tongue

Aspirin and whisky
Blessed whisky

Opening arteries
Thinning the blood

Prising off that
Cold hard

Hand on heart

Old

Let me die an old man's death
Let me linger long
In pain and ignominy
Soiling sheets
Humiliated by brisk nurses
Swearing, flailing
Wasted, wailing
Crinkled, wrinkled
Rumpled, crumpled
Drooling and forgetful
Give me time
Give me the time I need
To say goodbye
Give others the chance
To say what they must
There's nothing neat
Or dignified in this
Only the give and take
Of love and fear
Loss is coming
It's almost here.

Meditation

I don't meditate
I walk the dog
And sometimes throw a frisbee
Or a ball
That's all

I don't meditate
I read books
But not while walking
You may laugh
I'm not daft

I don't meditate
I ride a motorbike
Very carefully
I find
This soothes my mind

I don't meditate
I balance
I listen to ticking valves
I swerve and lean
Become the machine

I don't believe in fate
I concentrate
I don't meditate

Bag

Late May, and hospital time has merged with the searing brightness you get beyond 60 degrees north at this time of year to make sleep impossible. It's 6.00 am. I awoke from a vivid, strangely calming dream in which I was on a Boeing 747, empty apart from myself and the stewardess, who was insisting that I had to strap myself in for take-off. Despite the fact that I was stark naked and sitting in a canoe. Probably some unfulfilled fantasy. To be precise, it was a sit-on-top BIC Tobago polythene kayak, bungeed down to the fuselage. Come to think of it, it must have been a cargo 747, as there was nothing else inside it but me and the kayak. Why was there a stewardess, then? Listen, it was my dream. Such things are permitted.

Time to get up. I leave Susan and Dexter the Dog snoring peacefully and head downstairs, where the Green Bag awaits. 'Important: Patient's own Medicines' it says, capitalised exactly like that. I am the Patient. These Are My Medicines. If I Do Not Take Them I Will Die.

I should say that Dexter is new, and one of two dogs who share this decaying old house with Susan and myself. He is permitted to sleep at the bottom of our bed as he is relatively small, light and (mainly) aroma-free. The other dog, called Rug, is not, as she is very large, heavy, incredibly smelly and snores with the kind of reverberant, honking snort that makes you worried for your plasterwork. And I worry about our plasterwork anyway (old fashioned rotten laths and Georgian plaster, seeing as you're asking). Lulu, our last St Bernard, has left us now. She's buried in the back garden. Jim, the vet, came to give her one last injection. I

160

no longer borrow shotguns.

So, to stay alive I must take my pills, five in the morning and one very large one just before bedtime. An empty stomach is bad, so I usually have a piece of fruit and one of those Japanese yoghurt drinks full of digestion-aiding 'good bacteria' (just don't rub the stuff on an open wound). Before allowing a soluble aspirin to dissolve on my tongue, letting the bitter taste of wormwood coat my mouth with thoughts of absinthe, and swallowing Clopidogrel (aka Cloppy Doggerel), Atenolol, Candy Staton (aka Canesartan) and Lansoprazole with fresh Tropicana Florida orange juice, original with bits. Probably not that fresh, actually, but not so long in the tooth that it has assumed the dodgy fizziness of Bad Fanta. I will probably chase this down with an Omega Three Fish Oil capsule, just for the hell of it. That won't stop my dying, but it might, just might help keep me alive a minute or two longer. The day will end with an Atorvastatin the size of a Murray Mint, but less tasty.

Right now it's time to celebrate the prospect of the day, the anything-up-to-18-death-free hours that lie before me, barring accidents or undiagnosed problems. But I have been diagnosed to bits over the past month. Yea, verily, diagnosed almost unto death. And by the way, death, where is thy sting, while we're on the subject? Where is thy victory?

Oh, coming along soon enough, comes the reply. Don't you worry, son. I can wait. Time is on my side.

At this moment, time, thanks to modern pharmaceuticals, and some bizarre sci-fi surgery, is on my side. Everything's relative, of course. I'm looking at the next 18 hours with expectation, with hope, without any chest pain. It's a beautiful spring morning in the Shetland Isles. I am alive, with the prospect of a long, sunlit, cloud-laden, wind-whipped, hail-hammered day of life before me. Four seasons? And the rest. Meanwhile, it's time for coffee.

***   ***   ***

The beans, roasted just five days ago, are an espresso blend from The Bean Shop in Perth, currently my favourite supplier. Better than Avenue G and Artisan Roast in Glasgow, more reliable and faster when it comes to postage to this obscure outpost of our remote archipelago, they also supply Da (The) Peerie Shop Café in Shetland's capital Lerwick, run by my pal James Martin and an essential component in my Shetland life.

The internet has transformed life here. A postman told me last year that 70 per cent of his deliveries were now eBay-related, and broadband (fast and reliable in our neck of the bog, thanks to paying extra for BT Business) means a world of deliverable delights is available. And cheaply. Cheaper than local businesses can afford to retail at. Chuck in two chain supermarkets (Tesco and the Co-op) and some shops have struggled to survive. Clive's, once the most northerly and one of the best record shops in the UK, closed when the owner (whose name was, unsurprisingly, Clive Munro) found he could buy CDs and DVDs cheaper from Amazon and Tesco than he could order them from his normal wholesaler. The amazing thing was that many people still preferred to buy from him just because of his expertise and because they liked dealing with him. Brian Nicholson flourishes with his musical instrument shop High Level partly because Shetland is such a musical place, partly because he and his son Arthur offer beginner-to-expert lessons and also because buying a guitar or fiddle from High level means it will be set up properly, and chosen with care and concern for quality and performance.

Just like at The Last Bookshop. There's a model there for all retailers, I think, as all of Brian's prices can easily be beaten online. And mine.

On the other hand, I had to get some colour printing done the other day. Two thousand cross-folded leaflets, printed on both sides in full colour. The local printer, my former employer The Shetland Times Ltd, could do it for £418, collected from Lerwick and discounted, in case you're wondering, to the bone. An online concern called, ironically, alocalprinter.com – based in Cardiff – did it, including artwork alterations, for £336, including delivery, direct to The Last Bookshop.

TOM MORTON

***   ***   ***

This coffee is good. I have a Krups burr grinder and a Rancilio cappuccino machine, and I can provide you, should you be in the vicinity, with the best coffee in Shetland, if I can be bothered and my hand is steady enough. I can even make one of those wee leaf patterns in the foam. This morning I can't and my hand is a little shaky due to caffeine deprivation and the remnant of that stewardess/canoe/747 dream, so it's a quick microwaving of the milk and a single, not a double shot on top. My son James, who has been qualified as a doctor for, oh, four weeks now, insists that 'there is no link between caffeine consumption and cardiovascular events' but I don't like that feeling of the pump in my ribcage lurching from gentle rock'n'roll into a techno chattering, not when it's got bits of metal in there keeping the circumflex artery open. I mean, what happens if it goes into Hot Chip hard-house mode, ripping lumps of cholesterol off the walls of blood vessels, tearing the stent out of my artery and sending the whole heap of blood-borne detritus piling into my heart with a great clattering collision of innards, grunge and stainless steel? That's what all these pills are meant to prevent. Still, I don't want to put it to the test for a the sake of a cup of Java. I can live without the jolt I used to love so much of a morning. I can only live without that jolt, maybe.

Anyway, one shot is enough. Tasty. All pungent, toasty caramel and smoke, and yes, a mild kick. I take the cup outside and wander, barefoot, around the garden, the incredibly shrill-but-sweet song of *Troglodytes Troglodytes*, the Shetland wren, pursuing me, lifting my spirits higher than any caffeine shot ever could. And I think of Michael Harnett's wonderful poem *A Necklace of Wrens*, sent to me by Tim. The final stanza always leaves a mark:

That was when the craft came
which demands respect.
Their talons left on me
scars not healed yet.

IN SHETLAND

*** *** ***

This is the time of year for neither boats nor motorcycles. And yet, curiously, I feel the lack of both. As seriously bad weather begins to bite, the occasional day of clarity and calm invites the donning of leathers and a blast, at the very least, down to Brae for the papers and very possibly chips. I never would have believed it was possible to miss that winter biking chill, the seeping cold that infects your very bones, and can only be alleviated by means of deep frying, a peat-fired Rayburn, tea and whisky.

And there's a thing. I am currently forbidden the comfort of the solid fuel stove, due to well-founded suspicions that peat smoke may be triggering my increasingly-common asthma attacks. I am certain that the peat smoke used to malt the barley in my favourite whiskies has nothing to do with this ailment. At least, I hope not.

In fact it was one of those asthma attacks that rekindled my motorcycling desire, or as one eminent local has it "that irresistible disease". I thought to myself: why, at nearly 60 years old, am I not riding a motorbike due to fears of dying, when the only things standing between me and choking to death are a pair of inhalers, Covonia sweeties and a bottle of Benylin?

And so I find myself in that very pleasant state of 'considering a motorcycle'. In so many ways, this is better than actually owning one. Or two. Or three, as I did during one period of motorised disruption when I was storing the machines at two different locations in Shetland and one sooth in order to avoid domestic detection. Of course, I have to consider my age and decrepitude when examining the two-wheeled options. Running about dressed like a Power Ranger (do youngsters today even remember Power Rangers?) and bent in a curious shape over some plastic missile would not only be ridiculous, but hazardous to my arthritic bones and also extremely uncomfortable. There is the Harley-Davidson option, the last refuge of the elderly biker, but I have been there, dropped one at zero mph and been unable to get it back upright. The shame and embarrassment live with me still. The 'classic' BSA, Triumph or even MZ remains a possibility, were it not for my ineptitude with spanners and awful memories of using a mole wrench as a gear change for a month in Edinburgh on an old imitation Bonneville. Though there is something wonderful, as the American TV chatshow host Jay Leno once said, about a motorcycle you can actually see through, from one side to the other. On the other hand, the notion of bike that only works properly when it is leaking copious amounts of boiling oil onto your ankles is not particularly appealing.

Having done quite a lot of long-distance touring in my time, something that could permit the drop-of-a-hat setting out for faraway destinations such as, say, Wick, has its attractions. And then there is the adolescent fantasy of scooterdom. My first, off-road motorised two-wheel creature was a Vespa 150, ridden after dark on beaches and golf courses. But I fear I weigh too much these days for such a thing to achieve even the lowest of legal limits.

So I surf the net, contemplate Gumtree and Shetlink classifieds, and know for certain that were I to actually purchase that Kawasaki Versys (full service history and factory luggage, will deliver to Aberdeen) or BMW 1200GS-Ewen'n'Charley-Would-Be-Special, it would sit in the shed, eating up insurance money until spring.

But at least I'd have a motorbike. At least I'd be a motorcyclist.

As for floating things, well. I am a fully paid-up member of the Delting Boating Club, now with an empty berth in the marina at Brae. All through last winter I visited my boat, the *Happy Adventurer*, dealing with the issues that arise with all vessels left afloat during the dark and nasty months: the incursion of water, salt and fresh; bits falling off or blowing away (like the cabin roof, in my case), near-sinking, flat batteries and all the joys of having, as an old family friend once told me, a hole in the water you throw money into.

Now the *Happy Adventurer* has been sold, like our late pig Derek, to Thule, where it will doubtless be cared for and put to good use. I am boatless, then. Icy mornings skittering down the pontoons to hand-pump a Shetland Model two feet deep in rainwater are a thing of the past. And yet, and yet... I kind of miss it. Not as much as I miss not having a motorbike, admittedly.

Maybe I should buy a jetski. Or a snowmobile. Or a Scalextric set and one of those toy submarines that works on bicarbonate of soda. I could wear a lifejacket in the bath or full touring kit and helmet in the living room with my slot-car set. Or vice versa.

But no. At my age, that would be too dangerous.

*** *** ***

It was the last juicer in Shetland. Or the last one on retail sale, anyway, tracked down in the Hydro shop. I tried George Robertson's first, but there had been a rush on the things and orders were not due in for a week or two.

I'm not talking blender here, or food processor, or orange squeezer. A juicer is an electrical contraption which renders fruit and vegetables, from carrots to kale, broccoli (but not bananas, for some reason), separately into liquid and pulp. The idea is that drinking liquid (and kale juice is surprisingly palatable, especially with a wee bit of ginger added) can substitute for, well eating chips. And so you lose weight. I usually turn the pulp into soup, but that's another story.

The juicer is a gadget. Yet another gadget to add to the vast array that clutters up our kitchen, and indeed the entire house. I have a weakness for such objects. Indeed, some (especially my wife) would say I have an addiction to them. Like many males, I have a thing about them. About equipment, gear. Some would say it's a throwback to our hunter-gatherer origins, and the necessity of ensuring your spears, fishhooks and knives were all exactly fit for purpose. But I may have taken things a bit too far. From cameras to guitars, recording equipment through hi-fi to motorcycles and their acoustic variants. And, yes knives (oh, for a Wusthof!). I may have issues.

Take coffee, for example. As much coffee as possible, fresh, strong and made from freshly roasted beans. So coffee-obsessive did I become at one stage that I began having green (unroasted) beans shipped up from south and roasted them myself. I even contacted COPE when they closed their coffee-roasting operation at the late lamented Karabuni with a view to buying their unused machinery. (Perhaps fortunately for domestic harmony, I never heard back from them.) I did not buy a coffee roaster. I bought a popcorn maker and used it (flouting its design parameters) instead. Until the top melted.

It worked, but it was a tremendous, very messy faff and could go horribly wrong. Having said that, home-roasted fresh coffee beans are magical things. Especially when properly ground. And for that you need a burr grinder.

Not one of those, brutal, high-speed blade grinders (though I have one of those, a Moulinex, dedicated to grinding up fresh spices). A burr grinder is slower and does not destroy the, ahem, integrity of the grains of coffee. Or so they say. You can adjust the size of grain for the implement you are using to make the actual brew. Of course, I had to find one (Krups, who incidentally made nothing more aggressive than shavers during World War Two. It was Krupp who made the bad stuff.) And that is where things become slightly embarrassing.

At last count, in our kitchen, there were five active coffee-making options: Cafetiere, Hario V60 filter, Rancilio espresso maker, stovetop Bialetti, and Aeropress. Consigned to the washhouse is a Nespresso machine (The Great Evil) and an old Gaggia. I have never possessed the awful monstrosity my parents' used, an electric percolator, which used to boil the coffee for hours before it was served (as a treat) with Carnation milk.

Anyway, what I do possess seems more than enough. Obviously, all visitors to The Last Bookshop, which is not very far from said Kitchen, are free to avail themselves of this coffee making apparatus. Well, they're free to ask. And I'm free to say, och, just walk up to the hotel.

You will, of course, be familiar with the cafetiere, or French Press, first made famous in the UK courtesy of Michael Caine in the opening titles of the film *The Ipcress File*. As Susan and myself consume at least two mugs of strong coffee each before entering the outside world, that is the weapon of choice of a morning. On special occasions I will fire up the Rancilio, which is a semi-professional machine, second-hand and Italian in the same way an old Lamborghini is Italian. In other words, it needs careful attention, coaxing, mollycoddling and razor-sharp attention to detail to make it work. But, with the right roast and grind, and if it (and I) are in the right mood, it will produce the best cappuccino in Shetland. It's all about the crema. I will happily talk about the nature and pursuit of crema (the non-milky 'fake foam' atop an espresso) but would need several thousand words more than your already-trespassed-upon good nature, dear reader, would allow. I guess.

Stovetop Bialetti: that's one of those tightly-waisted aluminium pots that produce tar-like coffee with the ever-present risk of the silicon rubber seal twixt top and bottom adding a certain tyre-like quality. The Hario V60 is Japanese and a variant on the old-fashioned paper filter cone. You MUST use proper Hario filters and the Hario filter cone (preferably in ceramic) has patented grooves that can produce a silky-smooth drink. Though there are various pouring techniques that must be learnt first and you should really use a Hario long-spouted water pot and a thermometer. Oh, and mineral water!

Aeropress is my favourite. It's like a giant syringe with a disc of filter paper between the coffee and the hot water. It's fast, easy and makes a marvellous whooshing noise. And it can turn cheap supermarket grinds into something very acceptable. Meaning you don't have to roast beans or use the burr grinder...

I can tell that some of you are horrified at all this. Those who have had coffee at our house will be wondering why it didn't taste that special.

But then, that was the Nescafe we keep for visitors... and customers. Those special customers.

Dimming

Now comes the shortening of days, the change of light. A need to hoard and treasure the sun whenever it shows itself, peeking, low and slanting, as the planet's axis tilts and we feel the chill begin to creep into our fingers and toes.

Winter, but not quite. The all-encompassing, enclosing darkness of December is waiting, but in early November there is still the memory of October's amazing, unexpected warmth, a strange spurt of growth in the grass, a few stubborn leaves still clinging to brittle branches, the last migrant avian stragglers flung onto this remote rock on their flutter south.

This is the dimming of the year, a season without a name, beyond hairst, or autumn, before the grip of winter tightens. The days are long enough to get things done, and if the equinoctial blows aren't hammering in, you can work outside. As I write, I'm watching the painstaking repair of a drystane wall in the ancient cemetery near our house. It's slow, careful work, a buttressing of memory, a race against time. A battle against the dying of the year.

It's a battle against the dying of the year.

Time. What we have now is more than the fragile blink of illumination you get in the absolute depths of winter. There are hours to enjoy, to treasure the light, to reflect on the well-being it brings, in the knowledge that day by day, our allowance lessens. Faster, faster comes the darkness. But right now, the low angle of the sun makes the Shetland hills gleam, glitter and occasionally glower.

The clocks have flicked an hour backwards, and there is a sense of urgency about getting out of bed, so you can use the limited light, value it. You can feel the days diminishing, and this is a time of preparation: are the vehicles ready for the demands of The Big Dark and The Howling Cold? Lights, tyres (snow tyres, spare rims, even chains), anti-freeze. Shovel, rope. Spare gloves, an old anorak, just in case. Wellies, ice-insulated ones if you can afford them. Freezer trawler fishermen's boots are incredibly expensive but astonishingly warm.

The peats are in, the chimneys swept, tatties gathered (a bad year for potatoes, this; too warm, lots of pests). Central heating oil ordered, slates checked, for the gales are coming, rattling and rippling at the roof.

But there's still time, there's still enough of a day to get things done. To go for walks beyond the West Ayre to Burnside, up to Karaness, over to Gurnafirth. To snatch a cycle if it's not too windy, before the cold starts clutching at your chest with every breath.

And there is colour, too. Rainbows and radiation. The shallow rays and blustery squalls provide prismatic glories, while at night, the storm of solar restlessness lends our skies the shifting spectacle of Da Mirrie Dancers. The Northern Lights.

Light. We look for it, long for it, and relish it while we can. And yes, the winter will be long. But darkness has its own delights. As we will soon see...

Darkness

The translation of 'Up Helly Aa' is 'the lightening of the year', and there is indeed a sense, as the calendar lurches into a new twelvemonth, of spring beckoning, of winter's closed door opening to emit the merest chink of illumination.

The burning of torches and parade of torch-wielding guizers, the snarl of 'vikings' in stainless steel, Gore-Tex, composite and carbon fibre, the pungent aroma of kerosene, or paraffin if you prefer – does anyone remember the 'boom-boom-boom-boom' song which advertised Esso Blue, when every household had a paraffin heater and no-one, but the super-wealthy, central heating? Up Helly Aa is a shout of defiance at the darkness, a great celebration of community to speed spring on its way.

And not just in Lerwick. If you fancy seeing a Shetland viking fire festival up close and sometimes anorak-scorchingly personal, the 'country' festivals start in Scalloway before Lerwick's extravaganza and continue until the beginning of March. From Unst to Sumburgh, galleys are burnt, some at sea, and women participate on an (almost) equal footing, up to and including female Guizer Jarls at SMUHA – the South Mainland Up Helly Aa. Hall tickets are easier to come by, squad performances are often endearingly informal. These are smaller, very local festivals, but none the worse for that.

And for a period, what the various Up Helly Aas do is both signal the coming of the sun and intensify the darkness, exaggerate it. When the torches dim, when the galley embers burn low, you can walk back in the absolute blackness of a Shetland winter night, allow your eyes to adjust and enjoy the darkness.

Because Shetland's dark skies are a fabulous and often ignored asset. The Mirrie Dancers, the Northern Lights, are a much sought-after sight for visitors, and they are best enjoyed against the cold, clear inkiness of a sky unpolluted by streetlamps. You'll have seen the photographs, nearly all deceptively taken on hugely long exposures and utterly failing to capture the variety of the aurora's manifestations.

What's it really like? You may see only a vague greenish glow on the northern horizon. A flicker, a quiver in the air, sometimes accompanied – and only for a few people – by an insistent hum or buzzing noise. A vast, constantly shifting array of searchlight beams cutting clear white and green, pencil thin and massively wide. Great whirling crosses of colour, red, pink and green again, somehow oppressive and disturbing. Movement. It's as if the universe is restless. And of course, there's no predicting when, not really, although 'atmospheric conditions' and 'sunspot activity' may give you an indication. If the clouds don't intervene.

Connoisseurs of darkness, though, go for starlight. In very isolated places, the stars can play tricks. I woke up once in a tent, very far from the nearest road, camping in the first frosts of September. Outside, I looked up and was inside Vincent Van Gogh's The Starry Night, the famous painting of the view from his window in Saint-Rémy-de-Provence. The stars over Northmavine to me were as big as saucers, haloed and misty, with pin-sharp centres. Apart from the mutter of the waves and waterfalls at Lang Clodie Wick, it was completely silent, utterly still.

And the lightlessness of winter Shetland provokes parties, dances, but for me, best of all are the gatherings in stove-warmed houses, the telling of tales, the shivering and laughing at the mythical creatures of the past who may be lurking outside. But cannot come in as long as the whisky or rum is flowing and the fellowship is good. And then, when you have to walk home, you find that really, they were just stories all along, and the darkness is there to be enjoyed, to provide you with a new appreciation of this extraordinary environment.

So come and enjoy the Up Helly Aa of your choice. Surround

yourself with darkness, and look forward to the longer days. Take pleasure in the flash of fire, the flying sparks and defiant, flaming destruction.

But take time for the essential Shetland. The Black Stuff. Because it won't last. It never does.

Postscript

I hope you come to Shetland, if you've never been. I hope you find Ramnavine, Quidawick, Vronnafirth, Redskerry and the St Rognvald Hotel, and indeed The Last Bookshop. That you meet Ernest, and Roger, and Dean and Marjolein. There may be, by the time you get here, a Second Last Bookshop, as friends of ours are thinking of opening one on a very grand scale, in an old salmon hatchery. Sounds a bit fishy to me. It's way, way to the south of us. Hardly remote at all. Remotely civilised.

Some of you who are familiar with Shetland geography and nomenclature will be aware by now that I have taken some liberties with both. You may also suspect that some names have been changed in order not to cause local embarrassment. While others have been left with at least a little basis in reality, in order to cause local embarrassment. Maybe you're right. Maybe you're wrong. I couldn't possibly comment.

Lots of people have written lots of books about Shetland. This collection of musings and amusements doesn't even pretend to begin to scratch surface of the Old Rock. But maybe it does give a flavour of what it's like for someone to come here and find themselves in love – with a person, a place. To find themselves, after 30 years, at home.

Here I am, and here we are. Home. As I write this I am drinking a Beck's Blue non-alcoholic beer, looking at a piece of George Orwell's motorbike (salvaged from Barnhill on the Hebridean island of Jura, where he wrote 1984; but that's quite another story), wondering why I've just bought two Russian watches on eBay, and thinking about tonight's tea: supermarket quiche or... duck breasts.

All I have to do is go out and catch a duck.

I'm lying. I have supermarket duck breasts too. Today I drove to Lerwick for my regular heart check-up, and was sent away with slight concerns about my blood pressure and instructions not to drink more than one whisky a night. But the thing is, it's two years since that heart 'event' (I will not use the word 'attack'; nobody attacked anyone, nothing attacked nothing. Genetics narrowed my arteries and warned me to sort myself out. Or get someone else to sort me out). I'm still functioning, just about. Still walking about the place. Still exulting in this wild, windy, woolly, welcoming place.

Still wondering if 62 is too old for a motorbike. The final motorbike, the last motorbike. I look at that rusted lump of exhaust manifold, once handled by Eric Blair, and I promise myself: one last ride. One last power drive...

Here in The Last Bookshop, I can indulge my dreams, my fantasies, in the form of print. And that last impulse to buy a motorised two-wheeled machine has sent me searching the shelves for my beloved Hunter S Thompson's first and finest book, Hell's Angels. I may not be able to ride. But I can read.

And maybe I will ride too. I heard of someone in the South Mainland who's selling an old BMW. Susan doesn't have to know. I know somebody in Lerwick who'll hide it in their garage. But first, as the darkness falls and the promise of 'storm level' sunspot activity gives rise to hopes of an epic aurora, I think of Da Mirrie Dancers, the Northern Lights, and the walk that awaits me, later on.

I can walk. I can walk into a storm of light in the deepest darkness, here in the far north. Walk and remember, walk and dream.

And be at home.

1st April 2017, Quidawick
Stay at The Last Bookshop:
shetlandcrofthouseholidays.moonfruit.com

Follow The Last Bookshop and Tom on Twitter, Instagram and Facebook
@thebeatcroft
facebook.com/tommorton

Tom blogs, vlogs and flogs books, art, records, crafts and curios from The Last Bookshop at
thebeatcroft.co.uk

Some of the material in this book has previously been published, drastically mis-spelled, in The Shetland Times, Shetland Life, 60 North, Scottish Memories, Caught by the River and The Scotsman. Thanks are due to Susan, Jenny, Misa, Martha, Drew and Rayleen. And especially to Pauline, who refused to accept there was nothing wrong with me.

Made in the USA
San Bernardino, CA
14 August 2018